Political Leadership
and Collective Goods

NORMAN FROHLICH
JOE A. OPPENHEIMER
ORAN R. YOUNG

PRINCETON UNIVERSITY PRESS
PRINCETON, NEW JERSEY

1971

Political Leadership and Collective Goods

Publication of this book has been aided
by a grant from the Whitney Darrow Publication Reserve Fund
of Princeton University Press

This book has been composed in
Linotype Times Roman

*Printed in the United States of America
by Maple Press Company Inc.,
York, Pennsylvania*

To Peter Woodward
WHOSE INTELLECTUAL CURIOSITY
AND FRIENDSHIP WE MISS

Foreword

THE RATIONALITY OF
politics has always fired the imagination and defied the
solutions of men. Whom do we feel to be more instru-
mentally oriented than professional politicians? Still,
only Machiavelli has produced a work which pursues the
implications of rationality relentlessly in this field. In
doing so, Machiavelli became infamous because we were
all incapable of separating him from the effects to which
he told us the rationality of a political leader would lead.
One of the peculiarities implied by most savants who did
push any concept of rationality on the part of political
leadership was the apparent irrationality or arationality
of all other mankind. It sort of left one with the feeling
that were one a political leader, he'd be wicked, and
were he not, he'd be doltish. The only thing that saved
the field of politics from being a more dismal science
than economics was that it was hardly a science at all.

Through it all, down through the ages the general
public, hoi polloi, seemed to feel clearly that politicians were all too rational. They even seemed to hold
that followers were more easily explained as irrational
than as arational. After all, why should they not have
seen this clearly. "Politics" is so palpably concerned with
the tangible things of this world, especially with power
and pelf and with their reciprocals, responsibility, and
service.

These young social scientists may change all that beginning with this volume, for this volume only begins the

publication of their findings. They give us explicitly a profit-making theory of political leadership and political following. It is surprising how far they get with it and how much better this seems to fit the sense of hoi polloi about this aspect of human existence. Incidentally, they hold it to apply to all societies at all times—and if that's correct, it's bound to raise hob with some of our best ideological clichés. In this volume we have models based on rationality which begin to move us toward understanding in an area in which we feel instinctively that there is more rationality than has heretofore met the scholar. This is an especially refreshing possibility since most current preferences in the social science field seem to be for anti-intellectualism—almost as though the leitmotif were "to feel is to know"—as the preferred road to illumination. We can all agree that there is no knowing without feeling and evaluating even on the part of the coldest of fish among us, but I would assert that it is equally tenable to hold that there is no feeling or evaluating without some sort of knowing—or at least thinking. Certainly not in politics, anyway! After all, that is clearly implicit in our universal assumption that politics is always future oriented even when it is most conservative.

Frohlich, Oppenheimer, and Young seek to go to the most general level of analysis in all of this. What they are doing here—if it is successful—will have very far-reaching consequences for the soft social sciences of politics, anthropology, and sociology. The further development of this line of work may have important implications for the field of economics from which the muscle of its rigor springs. I also believe the models to be so arranged that they are not likely to prove trivially false— we shall learn a great deal from these young men even if they prove to be wrong. One has only to turn to pages

138–142, a recapitulation of the propositions put forth in this volume, to see that their hypotheses touch on a surprising number of the critical questions facing mankind—past, present, and future. If they prove to be correct and if their models and approach got them there, it's the head of the class for them and a new ball game for the rest of us. Most of us in the soft social sciences must learn to be obsolete joyfully.

MARION J. LEVY, JR.
Princeton University

Preface

WE ASK THE READER'S indulgence, for this book attempts to construct a general system of theory about political phenomena. Some readers may not be acquainted with the procedures associated with such constructions, and they will find the mode of discussion foreign. We would, therefore, like to offer some explanations concerning the procedures that we have adopted.

The construction of a general system of theory requires that assumptions be made. The assumptions both define the phenomena which are to be theorized about and enable the theorist to discover the interrelationships between these phenomena. The empirical content of a theory is set by the assumptions that are made. We hope that the assumptions we have chosen are "close enough to political reality" so that the ensuing model is a useful analogue to political phenomena of interest to social scientists.

Our central concern here, however, is with the logical interrelationships among the assumptions (i.e. the deductive aspects of the model), rather than with an analysis of its "fit" as an analogue to particular political phenomena. This is especially true of the early chapters of the book. But, as indicated in the concluding chapter, we are interested in explanations, and feel that we have identified explanations for a number of political phenomena. For example, we feel that we now have an explanation of why political leadership arises.

The construction of a general system of theory often begins with a restricted model which gradually is developed into a more general formulation. This permits the analytic identification of the effects of each complicating factor. Thus, our model begins with many important restrictions. We have been able, however, to attain some generalizations from our model, and Chapter Six suggests additional possibilities for generalization.

Our theory, like any other, is not restricted to a particular empirical case, such as the politics of the United States. Rather, the cases to which the construct is to apply are those phenomena which best conform to the definitions and assumptions of the model.

We have employed mathematics for the sake of precision, clarity, and efficient further development of the model. The mathematics we have used is simple and straightforward, and we have given verbal statements of all our results.

Finally, it should be noted that the ultimate test of a theory is its "fit" with reality, or how well its hypotheses predict the reality it purports to explain. We have not yet made any systematic effort to test the conclusions of our theory. Therefore, while we believe the theory to be logically sound, we are not now in a position to offer any conclusive statements about its correspondence with empirical realities. We would like to emphasize, however, that the model contains a number of predictive conclusions which are conceivably falsifiable and hence subject to corroboration or disproof.

This book is a joint project in every sense of the term, and it has been conducted on the basis of a fully equal partnership throughout. It represents the first fruits of a long-standing interest in deductive theory on the part of each of the authors and of a more recent working partnership among them. We hope to continue work along the same lines.

We should like to acknowledge that our work would not have been possible without the prior work of Mancur Olson, Jr. It was his book, *The Logic of Collective Action*, which first drew our attention to the problems associated with the supply of collective goods. In fact, our work began as an attempt to extend his theory directly and only gradually assumed its present form. Olson demonstrated the fruitfulness of treating the substance of politics as a problem in the demand and supply of collective goods. Moreover, his work indicates both the possibility and utility of analyzing problems of collective goods from an axiomatic perspective. Besides the inspiration offered by his work, we should like to thank him for his personal encouragement and valuable suggestions concerning revisions.

Beyond this, we owe an intellectual debt to Anthony Downs whose book, *An Economic Theory of Democracy*, is an important milestone in the search for deductive theories about political phenomena. Even though he has little to say about collective goods and we disagree with him on many issues, Downs's emphasis on role differentiation in the analysis of politicians and ordinary citizens has had a far-reaching impact on our own thinking.

Our thinking on this project was stimulated and refined during the academic year 1968–1969 by participation in a Faculty-Student Colloquium held at Princeton University. Although the substantive focus of the Colloquium was nominally on problems of international relations, its fundamental orientation was toward the prospects of constructing deductive theories in the field of political science. Our thanks go to both the Woodrow Wilson School of Public and International Affairs and the Center of International Studies at Princeton for supporting this Colloquium.

We owe a special debt of gratitude to Marion J. Levy, Jr., for supporting our interest in deductive theory; for coming to the defense of such theory whenever it was attacked as impossible, irrelevant, or undesirable in the field of political science; for identifying a number of weaknesses in earlier versions of the theory; and for ways which defy identification.

Several other acknowledgments are also in order. Edward L. Morse read the first drafts of this book and offered a number of helpful suggestions. William J. Baumol and Manfred Halpern went over some of our earlier formulations and, through their criticisms, prodded us to think over more carefully our position on a number of issues. For her unfailing optimism, which was a source of encouragement in our darker moments, we wish to thank Mrs. Darwin Luntz. We should also like to express our appreciation to the members of the secretarial staff of the Center of International Studies who did their usual magnificent job in reproducing our manuscript despite the strange mathematical symbols they found sprinkled throughout. Finally, it is a pleasure to acknowledge the debt we owe our wives: their criticism of our earlier drafts was surpassed only by the support they offered at key moments.

NORMAN FROHLICH
JOE A. OPPENHEIMER
ORAN R. YOUNG
Princeton, New Jersey
June 1970

Contents

Political Leadership
and Collective Goods

Introduction

WE DEFINE A COLLECTIVE
good as any good that cannot be withheld from any
member of a specified group once it is supplied to one
member of that group.[1] Two characteristics of collective
goods are immediately important. First, collective goods
are generally costly to supply. This is so whether the
good in question is defense, law and order, clear air,
or a bridge over a major river.[2] Second, collective goods
cannot be supplied through market mechanisms in a
social structure. Market mechanisms are defined in terms
of the supply of goods to individuals on an exclusive
basis, a characteristic that runs directly counter to the
emphasis on nonexclusion in the definition of a collective
good. As a result, collective goods must be supplied
through procedures or arrangements other than market
mechanisms. This is where the analysis of collective
goods impinges on the study of politics since the procedures suggested over the years for the provision of
such goods have often accorded a leading role to governmental mechanisms. This is especially true of collective
goods such as defense and law and order, which are
generally regarded as critical to the maintenance of viable societies.

The supply of collective goods has traditionally been

[1] This definition follows closely the discussion in Mancur Olson, Jr., *The Logic of Collective Action* (Cambridge 1965),
esp. 14.

[2] This would even be true of a negatively valued good such
as terror.

3

a major concern of political theorists. David Hume, for example, was already arguing in the eighteenth century that

> . . . two neighbors may agree to drain a meadow, which they possess in common; because it is easy for them to know each other's mind; and each must perceive, that the immediate consequences of his failing in his part, is the abandoning of the whole project. But it is very difficult, and indeed impossible, that a thousand persons should agree in any such action; it being difficult for them to concert so complicated a design, and still more difficult for them to execute it; while each seeks a pretext to free himself of the trouble and expense, and would lay the whole burden on others. . . .[3]

Hume proposed the introduction of "political society" as a solution for this dilemma, but he never explained the process through which political society would come into existence. More recently a group of economists with strong interests in political problems (such as Baumol, Olson, and Samuelson) have applied the tools of economics to the problem of analyzing the supply of collective goods in social structures. These writers have generally stressed the difficulties of achieving an adequate supply of collective goods. As Olson has summarized the central dilemma, ". . . even if all of the individuals in a large group are rational and self-interested, and would gain if, as a group, they acted to achieve their common interest or objective, they will still not volun-

---

[3] This passage is from David Hume, *A Treatise of Human Nature*. It is quoted in William J. Baumol, *Welfare Economics and the Theory of the State*, 2nd ed. (Cambridge 1967), 159.

tarily act to achieve that common or group interest."[4]

Several mechanisms have been suggested from time to time through which this dilemma may be broken. First, it has been suggested that if any given group or social structure contains a single individual who values the collective good in question more than its cost, such an individual will provide it for himself, thereby providing it for the other members of the group as well. Second, the members of a group may be forced to contribute to the provision of a collective good through some form of coercion. This solution is generally associated with the concept of government, but it need not be restricted solely to governmental mechanisms. Third, it has been suggested that there are cases in which the members of a group can be induced to contribute to the supply of a collective good if they receive some positive, private-good payoffs at the same time. This is the idea behind Olson's "by-product" theory of the provision of collective goods by various interest groups.

It is at this point that we wish to take up the argument in this book. First, we want to find out whether one or more of the mechanisms referred to in the previous paragraph are in fact necessary for the supply of collective goods in social structures. Second, we want to ques-

[4] Olson, *op.cit.*, 2. This argument leads to the conclusion that groups will often fail to organize to achieve their common interests in the supply of collective goods. And in cases where a group is already organized, this pattern of individual motivation gives rise to the so-called free-rider problem. That is, individuals will attempt to enjoy the benefits of a collective good without contributing to its supply.

Olson draws a distinction between small groups and large groups in this connection. We do not draw such a distinction. The details of our argument on this issue are set forth in Appendix 1.

tion whether these conditions are sufficient to insure the supply of collective goods. Third, we want to analyze the process through which any mechanism for the supply of collective goods is established. Except in the unusual case of the single individual who supplies a collective good, it is generally agreed that some sort of organization is required to collect resources and to supply the good in question. Yet discussions of collective goods seldom pay much attention to the process through which such an organization can or will come into existence in a social structure.

The missing link in all this analysis seems to us to be the concept of political leadership or political entrepreneurship.[5] If individuals are rational and self-interested and the provision of collective goods requires an organization, such goods will be supplied when someone finds it profitable to set up an organization (or make use of some existing organization), collect resources, and supply the goods in question. Any individual who acts to supply a collective good without providing all of the resources himself we will call a *political leader* or *political entrepreneur*.[6] Such an individual will only find this

[5] The concept of political entrepreneurship has been the subject of a growing body of literature. Works on the subject include: Richard Wagner, "Pressure Groups and Political Entrepreneurs," *Papers on Non-Market Decision Making* 1 (1966), 161–170 (a review of Olson, *op.cit.*); Robert H. Salisbury, "An Exchange Theory of Interest Groups," *Midwest Journal of Political Science* 13 (1969), 1–32; and Albert Breton and Raymond Breton, "An Economic Theory of Social Movements," *The American Economic Review* 59 (1969), 198–205. Suggestive as these works are, they do not culminate in a comprehensive theory of political entrepreneurship regarding the supply of collective goods. This will be discussed further in Chapter One.

[6] In this book we define politics to include all those phenomena associated with the supply of collective goods in a social structure.

role valuable when the total resources he can collect as a leader exceed his costs, thereby producing a leader's surplus.[7] Political leaders will have four potential sources of revenue from contributions.[8] In the first instance, the members of the social structure may contribute directly for the supply of the collective good. Such contributions, made on a voluntary basis, are called *donations*. Resources extracted through the use of collectively threatened sanctions are called *extortions*. In addition, members may contribute through private-good changes with the leader. We will label such contributions *purchases* when they are made in exchange for positively valued private goods and *taxes* when they are made to gain freedom from individualistically threatened sanctions expected as a consequence of failure to contribute.[9] At the same time, political leaders will always have two types of cost: the cost of supplying the collective good, and the cost of providing a collection organization.

One consequence of this should be emphasized here:

[7] This surplus must be larger than the utility the potential leader can hope to gain from other activities. Any individual who chooses to occupy the role of political leader must give up a variety of other options. Rational leaders will opt for such leadership roles, therefore, only when the surplus they can achieve compares favorably with the utility they can obtain from other roles in the social structure.

[8] In this discussion, we leave out the impact of noncontributed revenue accruing to the leader from various sources. The effects of these factors will be discussed explicitly in Chapters One and Two.

[9] Two dimensions underlying this classification of sources of revenue are particularly important. First, there is the distinction between contributions for collective goods and contributions for private goods. Second, there is the distinction between contributions made for the supply of positively valued goods (i.e. donations and purchases) and those made to avoid the imposition of negatively valued sanctions (i.e. extortions and taxes).

7

an individual may rationally occupy a leadership role
and supply a collective good to a group even if he does
not value the good or even if he values the good negatively. We would, therefore, predict that some leaders
of organizations do not value the goals of the organization. So long as he can achieve a leader's surplus, his
personal valuation of the good may be of little consequence. It is the political leader's motivation for profit
that accounts for the development of a collection organization and the supply of collective goods.

This line of thinking raises additional questions. Once
an individual occupies a political leadership role and
provides organization for a group, what are his objectives? We assume that a rational political leader will
attempt to maximize his surplus. He will do so regardless
of how he wishes to use his surplus, and he can be expected to change his positions on specific substantive
issues as a function of their changing profitability.

But what insures that a leader will supply a collective
good in the promised quantities rather than exploiting
the members of the group through coercive extortion
or taxation? Once an individual is securely established
in a leadership role, he has incentives to increase his
surplus through the application of sanctions and through
cheating on the provision of collective goods. There are
several factors that counteract these incentives and set
limits on a leader's ability to exploit the members of
his group. First, he cannot force the members below
the level of healthy subsistence without reducing their
productivity and, therefore, their ability to offer him contributions. Second, exploitation based on sanctions is
likely to reduce the size of the donations that individual
members of the group make on a voluntary basis. As
the leader increases his revenues through the use of sanctions or reduces the supply of collective goods, the ra-

tional individual will experience a decline in his incentive to contribute voluntarily to the provision of such goods. Third, and potentially of greater importance, political competition may limit the leader's ability to exploit the members of the group. Other things being equal, the incentives for nonleaders to become competitors for the leadership role increase as the size of the leader's surplus expands. The rational political leader, therefore, will have to take several factors into account in calculating the prospects of increasing his surplus by raising the levels of extortion and taxation or by reducing the supply of collective goods.[10]

This conclusion leads us to a more systematic examination of competition for leadership roles in social structures. In this connection, the first point to notice is that political competition is a collective good in itself. Thus, the origins and the supply of political competition can be explained in terms of the same analysis as that outlined above in connection with the emergence of political leaders. Competition will be supplied in a social structure when some individual finds it profitable to do so. Such competition, however, can take two forms. First, a competitor may attempt to achieve a leader's surplus on the same basis as the original leader by supplying a different set of collective goods to the group. Second, a competitor may try to replace an incumbent leader, thereby becoming a direct opponent for the incumbent's role.

It is useful to contrast competition among suppliers of collective goods with competition among suppliers of private goods. In the case of political competition,

---

[10] Another potential limitation on the leader's ability to exploit is the possibility that members can leave the group. It will not be possible to analyze this possibility in formal terms, however, until we extend our model to cover exclusion mechanisms as suggested in Chapter Six.

9

direct opposition is especially important. The opponent's role premise is very similar to that of the political leader in analytic terms, but the introduction of opposition has a substantive impact on the situations of the incumbent leader and the ordinary members of the group. Given the presence of an opponent, the incumbent must consider the prospect that he may not remain in the leadership role indefinitely. He must therefore think about the problem of maximizing his surplus over some specific period of time. Similarly, the ordinary member of the group must decide how to allocate his donations among the competitors as well as how much to donate in total. In general, however, the emergence of an opponent to an incumbent leader will not necessarily minimize or even reduce the extent to which the members of the social structure are exploited. If the emergence of opposition is to reduce exploitation, competition must be continuous and it must be able to maintain itself without relying on coercion.

Underlying the analysis of many of the questions raised in this Introduction is the problem of strategic interaction. Strategic interaction refers to the behavior of two or more individuals whenever the choices of each are contingent upon his estimation of the choices of the other(s). The actual amount of any given collective good an individual receives is heavily influenced by the contributions of other members of the group because of the collective nature of the good in question. As a result, every member will pay close attention to the actual choices of others and to the probabilities associated with such choices in future time periods in calculating his expected value from any given contribution on his part. Strategic interaction will therefore play an important role in situations involving the supply of collective goods. In the absence of competition, strategic interactions will occur both among the ordinary members of the group and between the ordinary members and the political leader. With the introduction of political competition, such interactions will also take place between the incumbent leader and his opponent(s) and between the opponent(s) and the ordinary members.

CHAPTER ONE

Noncompetitive Politics

A NUMBER OF THEORISTS have attempted to analyze political phenomena in terms of the concept of collective goods. The work of these theorists can be divided into two principal streams. The first focuses on difficulties that occur when individuals attempt to supply themselves with a collective good. This stream, which encompasses the majority of existing analyses of collective goods, concentrates on difficulties arising from the free-rider problem and tendencies for the supply of the goods to be extremely suboptimal.[1] The second stream emphasizes the introduction of the concept of entrepreneurship to augment the explanatory power of the original models to handle cases in which large groups apparently do receive meaningful amounts of collective goods.[2]

We begin this chapter with a brief account of these two streams of analysis, together with a discussion of their shortcomings as the basis of a consistent explanation of the supply of collective goods. This will set the

[1] The relevant literature on this subject dates back many years. Nonetheless, economic analysis of the collective-goods problem took a new turn when Paul Samuelson published "The Pure Theory of Public Expenditure," *Review of Economics and Statistics,* 36 (Nov. 1954), 387–89. Additional work has since been done on several aspects of the problem. In this context, note especially the contributions of Mancur Olson, Jr., *The Logic of Collective Action* (Cambridge 1965), and James Buchanan, *The Demand and Supply of Public Goods,* (Chicago 1968).

[2] This literature is cited in footnote 5 of the Introduction.

stage for our effort to construct an alternative model to explain political phenomena in terms of the activities of entrepreneurs who act to supply collective goods.

THE PROBLEMS INHERENT IN THE SUPPLY OF COLLECTIVE GOODS

Let us assume that the resources required to supply a given collective good (X_i) exist, that the members of the social structure, as a group, value the good more than the cost of supplying it, but that each member values any additional unit of the good less than the previous unit (i.e., the members experience declining marginal utility with respect to the supply of the good).[3] Assume also that the individual members of the group behave in a rational and self-interested manner. In such situations, the question of how the collective good can be supplied is not a trivial one. To the extent that the good is collective in nature, it is possible for individuals to receive it even if they do not contribute toward its supply. Consequently, individuals acting in a self-interested fashion will experience incentives to withhold their own contributions, hoping that the efforts of others will be sufficient to provide the good to the whole group.[4] And under certain circumstances, these responses (described in this discussion as free-rider tendencies) can jeopardize the supply of the collective good altogether.[5]

[3] See Appendix 2 for an explanation of the symbols used throughout the text.

[4] A more formal treatment of this problem is set forth in Norman Frohlich and Joe A. Oppenheimer, "I Get By With a Little Help from My Friends," *World Politics*, 23 (Oct. 1970), 104–120.

[5] We employ the phrase "free-rider tendencies" in a broad sense. Specifically, we apply the phrase to situations involving incentives to enjoy a collective good without contributing to its supply. These may prevent the group from supplying itself with the good altogether.

13

Interactions Among Consumers

The first stream of analysis concentrates on interactions among prospective consumers of any given collective good. The theorists who have contributed to this stream make a key distinction between large groups and small groups at the outset, and they emphasize the problems of supplying collective goods to large groups.[6] Their analysis leads them to conclude that the provision of collective goods to large groups is a major political problem. Specifically, their argument leads to the conclusion that some groups of individuals who value a collective good more than the cost of providing it will not, in fact, be able to supply it to themselves in any meaningful amount.

To illustrate this analysis in greater detail, let us summarize the argument of Mancur Olson, whose formulation is probably the best known and most powerful in this stream of analysis. Olson argues that two fundamentally different situations are possible in large groups. First, one or more members of the group may value the good more than the cost of supplying it. Here Olson argues that there is a presumption that some of the good will be supplied, at least over a period of time. Second, no individual member of the group may value the good

[6] Group size is related to the collective-goods problem in two distinguishable ways. First, it is argued that the size of the group will have an impact on the importance of free-rider tendencies. Second, group size is said to determine the degree of suboptimality in cases where some of a collective good is supplied.

Nevertheless, it is argued in Appendix 1 as well as in Frohlich and Oppenheimer, *op.cit.*, that the size of the group is not a crucial factor governing the supply of collective goods. In our own analysis of the supply of collective goods, therefore, we do not differentiate groups with respect to size.

14

more than the cost of supply. In this case, Olson concludes that the good will ordinarily not be supplied in the absence of indirect incentives. Let us briefly sketch the arguments underlying these conclusions.[7]

Consider first the case in which one or more members of the group, as individuals, value the good more than the cost of supply. Simply stated, Olson's argument here is that the whole group will eventually receive some of the good because the individual who values it more than the cost of supply will realize that the other members of the group regard contributions on their part as unnecessary and act to maximize his own utility by purchasing the good. That is, any individual who values the good more than the cost of supply will act to maximize his own utility with respect to the good, thereby supplying some of it to the group as a whole, as soon as he realizes that he cannot rely on the contributions of others to achieve this result.[8]

When a collective good is supplied through this procedure to a large group, however, the level of supply will be distinctly suboptimal from the perspective of the group as a whole.[9] This follows directly from the collective nature of the good. If one member of the group purchases some of the good because he is able to maximize his personal utility by doing so, every other mem-

[7] The details of Olson's argument can be found in Olson, *op.cit.,* 1–65.

[8] Due to the effects of bargaining, an individual who values the collective good more than the cost of supply may not act to provide the good at first. But Olson argues that this condition is not likely to persist indefinitely (*ibid.,* 49–50).

[9] Suboptimality of supply refers to any situation in which some of a given collective good is supplied but the recipients could share the cost of additional units in some way that would allow some of them to become better off with the purchase of more of the good while no one suffers.

15

ber of the group will receive these units at no cost. Given this free access to the units of the good purchased by the first individual, others (who are assumed to experience declining marginal utility with respect to the good) will have a reduced incentive to purchase additional units of the good. This means that as those who place the highest value on the good buy additional units, the other members of the group will remain free riders. Sooner or later the cost of purchasing an additional unit of the good will outweigh the utility accruing to any member of the group from such a purchase. At this point, no more units of the good will be purchased, and those who placed a relatively low value on the original units will enjoy those units provided by their more zealous neighbors.

It is clear, however, that the value of an additional unit of a collective good to the group as a whole is not the same as its value to the individual member who purchases it. On the contrary, the value of an additional unit of a collective good to the group is the sum of the values placed on that unit by the individuals who will receive it in the event that it is supplied. And in large groups, this aggregate value will usually be far greater than the value placed on the good by any individual member. Consequently, whenever the cost of purchasing the next unit of a collective good is borne by a single individual (who weighs only his private costs and benefits), the outcome will be far from optimal from the perspective of the group as a whole. In fact, when the group is very large, the good may be so suboptimally supplied that the situation is virtually equivalent to the nonsupply of the good.[10]

[10] See also Olson's discussion of this problem in *ibid.*, 48–49, n68.

16

Now consider the second case in which no individual member of the group values the good more than the cost of supply. Here Olson concludes that the prospects for supplying the collective good to a large group, in the absence of indirect incentives, are even worse. Thus, he argues that each individual in such a group will feel that a contribution from him will be of negligible importance in securing the collective benefit. That is, each member will feel personally inefficacious because he concludes that the impact of a donation from him will be insignificant and because he sees no way of coordinating his decisions with those of the other members of the group. Accordingly, all the members of the group will decide that it is irrational for them to contribute to the supply of the collective good, and the group will fail to supply itself with the good.

In both cases, therefore, Olson reaches the conclusion that large groups will fail to supply themselves with meaningful amounts of valued collective goods in the absence of indirect incentives. Given this analysis of the collective-goods problem, Olson and others have attempted to identify mechanisms through which meaningful amounts of collective goods can still be supplied to large groups. Specifically, they argue that the dilemma can be resolved by the introduction of indirect procedures such as the collection of resources through a coercive mechanism or the use of private-good incentives. But these constructs are not sufficient to form the basis of a consistent explanation of the supply of collective goods to large groups. For example, what is to prevent an individual who has collected resources through coercion or through positive, private-good incentives from absconding with the resources without supplying the collective good or using the resources for some

17

purpose other than the provision of the collective good? Afterall, any mechanism designed to insure that the resources collected were actually applied toward the supply of the good would be a costly collective good itself, benefiting the same individuals who were scheduled to receive the original collective good. Similarly, why should individuals pay more than a market price for private goods if they are unwilling to make voluntary contributions toward the supply of the collective good? These inadequacies leave the developers of the first stream of analysis of the collective-goods problem without a sufficient explanation of the provision of meaningful amounts of collective goods to large groups.

The Concept of Entrepreneurship

The basic structure of these arguments concerning the supply of collective goods has been supplemented by the work of another group of analysts.[11] These scholars have been attracted to the collective-goods problem by various empirical situations in which collective goods are apparently supplied to large groups as well as by the abstract models associated with the first stream of analysis. In essence, this second stream has introduced the notion of a supplier of collective goods. That is, these analysts posit the existence of an entrepreneur who makes a profit of one kind or another from the activities involved in supplying collective goods to a large group. Wagner, for example, attempts to demonstrate that mechanisms other than the activities of interest groups can account for the achievement of collective benefits by emphasizing the role of political entrepreneurs in

[11] See footnote 5 of the Introduction for citations of the relevant literature.

18

democratic political processes. Such entrepreneurs, he argues, supply collective benefits in exchange for some "political profit." Salisbury concentrates initially on the role of the entrepreneur in establishing and maintaining interest groups, and he goes on to suggest that the concept of political entrepreneurship could be extended to explain a variety of phenomena associated with political leadership more broadly construed. And Breton and Breton refer to the role of "social entrepreneurs" who provide social movements to groups of individuals who find that their income is declining relative to their expectations.

Each of these analysts has attempted to sketch in an alternative explanation for the supply of positively valued collective goods by introducing the concept of entrepreneurship. In each case, however, this work is based on an ambiguity: it is not clear that there is any incentive or motivation for the individual members of a group to make contributions toward the supply of any given collective benefit. On the contrary, there often appears to be an implicit assumption to the effect that individuals will feel such a great sense of personal inefficacy concerning the supply of the collective benefits that they will not be willing to make any contributions to an entrepreneur to facilitate the supply of the good. Consequently, the entrepreneur is sometimes depicted as a quasi-economic entrepreneur who sells access to sets of benefits on an individualistic basis at a price. And at other times, he seems to be a provider of genuine collective goods who obtains a profit in some unspecified fashion from contributions made by the members of the group. But so long as the assumption of individual inefficacy holds, there is no way of linking the supply of collective goods and the achievement of a profit by an entrepreneur. Unless the individual feels that a contribu-

19

tion on his part to an entrepreneur will make a difference with respect to the supply of the collective good, he will have no incentive to make such a contribution, and the entrepreneur will be deprived of his source of profits.

Reconsidering the Problem

The concept of entrepreneurship, therefore, is not adequate to account for the supply of genuine collective goods unless there is some way to generate resources for the supply of these goods. Moreover, we have shown that contributions for the supply of collective goods on the part of rational, self-interested individuals cannot be explained solely by reference to the notions of coercive mechanisms and private-good incentives. Accordingly, insofar as collective goods are supplied to large groups in meaningful amounts, there must be some reason for individuals to contribute toward the supply of the collective goods themselves. That is, at least some members of the group must estimate that contributions on their part can make a worthwhile difference in facilitating the supply of the collective goods.

Whenever the supply of a collective good is at stake, the efficacy of a contribution by any given member of the group will be a function of the behavior of the others with respect to their contributions. This follows from the collective nature of the good. But the behavior of each of the others will be influenced, in turn, by his expectations concerning the behavior of a subgroup composed of all the members of the group other than himself and including the first individual. Consequently, each member of the group will find that his sense of personal efficacy (or inefficacy) concerning contributions for the supply of the collective good will be predicated upon expectations regarding the behavior of others, and prob-

20

lems associated with the phenomenon of reflexive reasoning or strategic interaction can be expected to occur.[12] In this context, it seems necessary to allow for a variety of possible patterns of expectations on the part of each member of the group concerning the coordination of his actions with the actions of the other members. When all the members of the group feel inefficacious with respect to their own contributions, expect the others to feel the same way, and do not expect that a donation on their part would change the feelings of the others, the problems described by Olson and others arise in their severest form. When other patterns of expectations predominate, on the other hand, rational individuals may

[12] Note that this formulation of the individual's calculations differs from the view of individual decision-making in large groups which is widely employed in microeconomics. Thus, the models of microeconomics often assume that each individual (or firm) will face a fixed price or a horizontal demand curve because he is only one among a large number of actors; the impact of his own actions will be so insignificant that it will not be "noticeable" to the other members of the group, and he cannot hope to coordinate his actions successfully with those of others. For an effort to extend this type of reasoning to the collective-goods problem see Olson, 44–52. We do not make such an assumption, however, in our analysis of the problems associated with the supply of collective goods. Whether or not it is justifiable in the context of microeconomics, we do not see any persuasive reason to make such an assumption in dealing with the political problems generated by efforts to supply collective goods to large groups. Not only does the collective nature of the goods accentuate the impact of each member's actions on the choices of the others, it is also the case that various coordination mechanisms, such as political leaders or parties, may play a role in determining the expectations the individual members of the group ultimately form of each other's probable behavior with respect to contributions toward the supply of collective goods. A more formal discussion of our position on this issue can be found in Chapter Five.

21

conclude that it is worthwhile to contribute toward the supply of the collective good.

Nevertheless, such contributions are likely to remain very limited unless some mechanism is established to allow the members of the group to share the marginal costs of purchasing units of the good.[13] With the introduction of a marginal-cost-sharing arrangement, however, it is possible to imagine situations in which individuals who feel efficacious would be willing to contribute amounts up to the value they place on the units of the good at stake. Thus, in large groups in which no one values the collective good more than the cost of supply, it becomes possible for the members to pool their resources so that the good can be supplied through a central agency. Moreover, the possibility of marginal cost sharing means that extreme suboptimality need not occur in groups in which one or more individuals value the good more than the cost of supply. That is, additional units of the good can be supplied through the pooling of resources either from the outset or, in any case, after individuals have stopped purchasing units of the good in their private capacity.

To appreciate fully the combined impact of personal feelings of efficacy and the possibility of introducing marginal-cost-sharing arrangements, consider the situation of the individual member of the group in terms of his expected-utility calculations. An individual may feel that a contribution on his part toward the supply of the collective good is worthwhile because his contribution affects the probability that the good will be supplied and/or because it affects the quantity of the good sup-

---

[13] Without such a mechanism, individual members would not only be purchasing units of the good wholly out of their own resources, but they would also have no central agency that could function to pool their contributions.

plied. In deciding on his own contribution (if any), each individual must estimate what others will contribute, taking into account the fact that their decisions will be influenced, in turn, by estimates of the probable behavior of a subgroup of which he is a member. Under the circumstances, the individual member will contribute whenever he expects others to make contributions toward the provision of the good which, when combined with his own contribution, will leave him better off than if he had decided not to contribute.[14] Note that situations of

[14] Given this formulation of the calculations of the individual, it is unnecessary to distinguish between groups in which at least one individual values the good more than the cost of supply and groups in which this is not the case. To illustrate this point, assume that a group contains an individual who values the collective good more than the cost of supply. There is no guarantee that this individual will supply any of the good to the group, since he may estimate that he can receive the benefits of the good while letting others pay for it. In general, the behavior of such an individual will depend upon his estimations of the probable behavior of the other members of the group because of the collective nature of the good in question. If, for example, an individual valued a given collective good at the utility equivalent of $100 while the good cost only $10 to supply, we could not conclude that he would certainly pay the cost of supplying the good, thereby obtaining a "profit" of $90. On the contrary, this individual would weigh the following alternatives: (1) pay the $10 and obtain the equivalent of $90 with a probability of one, or (2) pay nothing and obtain an expected-utility payoff of $100P_j(X_i)$, where $P_j(X_i)$ is his estimate of the probability that the good will be supplied by others even in the absence of a contribution on his part. Only if $90 > $100P_j(X_i)$ or $.9 > P_j(X_i)$ would we expect such an individual to supply the collective good himself. We would therefore expect to find some individuals who value a collective good more than the cost of supplying it and yet refrain from contributing toward its supply.

In fact, such an individual would have additional options. He might contribute some amount less than the total cost of

23

this kind will generate strategic interaction since the decisions of the members of the group will be reciprocally contingent upon each other. Accordingly, it is to be expected that the members of the group will experience some difficulty deciding whether to contribute toward the supply of the collective good, and there may be room for bargaining while the members are in the process of making their decisions.[15] Nevertheless, at the time he makes his final decision concerning his contributions, each individual must plug some estimates of the probable behavior of the other members of the group into his expected-utility calculations.[16]

In the absence of any mechanisms for the coordination of expectations and the pooling of resources, it is highly likely that the members of the group will act in such a way as to fail to supply themselves with meaningful amounts of the collective good. When mechanisms of this kind do exist, however, the number of members of the group who consider it worthwhile to make a contribution toward the supply of the collective good will generally increase. And there is no decisive reason why these conclusions should be altered as the size of the group

---

supplying the collective good in the expectation that contributions from others would make up the difference necessary for the provision of the good. In such cases, the exact size of his contributions would be a function of his estimations of the probable actions of the other members of the group. In general, however, the calculations of such an individual are essentially the same in analytic terms as those of the members of a group in which no one values the collective good more than the cost of supplying it.

[15] For a formal discussion of strategic interaction which emphasizes the importance of this phenomenon in analyzing the supply of collective goods see Chapter Five.

[16] Note that in order to make any decision at all, including the decision not to contribute, the individual must ultimately attach some probability estimates to the behavior of others, even if only tacitly or on the basis of simple rules of thumb.

increases.[17] Consequently, an examination of mechanisms for the coordination of expectations and the pooling of resources becomes a central issue in the analysis of the extent to which large groups will succeed in supplying themselves with collective goods.[18]

Whenever the members of a group find it worthwhile to contribute toward the supply of a collective good and perceive that a marginal-cost-sharing arrangement is possible, there may be a potential profit for an entrepreneur. Such an entrepreneur can establish a collection organization, gather the contributions, and provide the collective good. And so long as the resources he can collect in this manner exceed the cost of supplying the good, he can make a profit. In such cases, the crucial function of the entrepreneur is to provide a mechanism for the pooling of resources. Moreover, to the extent that the entrepreneur can act as a coordination mechanism by controlling or manipulating the expectations of the individual members of the group regarding the behavior of the other members (and therefore their sense of efficacy concerning their own contributions), his ability to make a profit may be enhanced. Such an individual would be acting as a political leader, supplying positively valued collective goods for a profit. The analysis which follows leads to a formal explanation of the interactions between consumers and suppliers of collective goods when at least some individuals feel that their contributions toward the supply of the goods will make a difference some of the time and when there is scope for sharing the marginal costs of supplying the goods through the introduction of some mechanism for the pooling of resources.

[17] Detailed explanations of this point can be found in Appendix 1 as well as in Frohlich and Oppenheimer, *op.cit.*

[18] Many of the activities of political parties, for example, can be meaningfully interpreted from this perspective.

A Formal Model of Noncompetitive Politics

The following assumptions and definitions are required for the construction of our model. Throughout this chapter and the next, we assume that there is no competition for occupancy of the leadership role. Subsequent chapters deal with situations that arise when there is political competition.

Behavioral Assumptions

All the arguments in this book are based on the assumption that individuals behave rationally. Rationality is defined in terms of the following three conditions: (1) the individual evaluates alternatives in his environment on the basis of his preferences among them; (2) his preference ordering is consistent and transitive; and (3) he always chooses the preferred alternative. For purposes of derivations, however, several subsidiary assumptions concerning rational behavior are required.

First, in order to analyze situations that involve risky alternatives, we assume that individuals evaluate their alternatives in terms of expected-value calculations. "Expected value" is here used in the technical sense to refer to the value one places on an event times the probability that the event will actually take place. This definition raises a problem: if people evaluate alternatives in terms of the benefits and the probability that the benefits will be received, how do people compare increases in probability to decreases in benefits? That is, what is the "trade-off function" between risk and benefit?

For example, assume an individual can choose one of two lottery tickets. The first one involves a large prize but a small chance of winning. The second involves a smaller prize but a greater chance of success. How is he to choose between the two alternatives? To get around

26

this difficulty, one must assume that the individual is willing to exchange some change in his chances of success for a change in the size of the prize. To reduce the problem to manageable proportions, we also assume an interval scale of utility. That is, if the first alternative is associated with a utility valuation of U_1 and a probability P_1 of being received, and the second with U_2 and P_2, then it is assumed that the individual will be indifferent as between alternatives one and two if $U_1P_1 = U_2P_2$. Note that this conception of utility does not assume interpersonal comparisons of utility.[19]

The second restriction on our formulation of rational behavior involves the notion of self-interest. The self-interest assumption requires that an individual, in evaluating his alternatives, does not give direct consideration to changes in the happiness of others caused by his actions. That is, the individual does not value the utility of others as an end in itself. This assumption does not rule out all considerations of the interests of other people. It restricts the individual's concern for others to their reactions to his actions, in contrast to changes in their utility unaccompanied by reactions. Suppose, for example, that the actions of one man make a second man unhappy. Given our assumption of self-interest, the first man will consider this effect of his actions only

[19] Daniel Bernoulli, "Exposition of a New Theory on the Measurement of Risk" (English translation by Louise Sommer of papers written in 1730 and 1731), *Econometrica* 22 (1954), 23–26. This conception of expected utility has been developed into its contemporary form by J. von Neumann and O. Morgenstern, *Theory of Games and Economic Behavior,* 2nd edn. (Princeton 1947). For straightforward summaries of these constructs, see the first appendix in R. Duncan Luce and Howard Raiffa, *Games and Decisions* (New York 1957) and Anatol Rapoport, *Fights, Games and Debates* (Ann Arbor 1960), 121–129.

if he expects the second man to react specifically to these actions in such a way as to affect the first man's utility.

Third, we assume that rational individuals operate under a number of constraints in attempting to maximize their utility. The most important of these constraints is the roles which the individual occupies. Since any individual occupies a number of roles and since he must maximize his utility with respect to the resultant set of roles rather than any single role, no individual will ever act solely in terms of a single role.[20] Under certain conditions, however, it is reasonable to expect a high degree of conformity to a specific role premise.[21] These conditions are: (1) that additional actions taken in terms of the specified role are more valuable to the individual in question than actions taken in terms of any other role, and (2) that the sources of the benefits and costs which accrue to the individual from the specified role are differentiated from other aspects of the environment.

Though the first condition is never completely met in empirical situations, it is sometimes approached through the application of sanctions against role occupants who deviate from their role premises. An individual may lose his occupancy of a role, for example, if he deviates from the role premise. If the role is a particularly valuable one, this will constitute a serious sanction. It is our belief that the leadership roles set

[20] T. Scitovsky, "A Note on Profit Maximization and Its Implications," *Review of Economics and Statistics*, 11 (1943), 57–60.

[21] We define a role premise as a particular set of aspects of the alternatives in terms of which an individual evaluates his utility. According to micro-economic theory, for example, the role premise of economic entrepreneurs is profit maximization. Thus, it is assumed that any individual entrepreneur will evaluate his alternatives in terms of their profitability.

28

forth in this model conform relatively well to this pattern. In this respect, they are analogous to the roles of the entrepreneur in the theory of the firm. The role of the member, however, is less subject to these constraints. It parallels the role of the consumer. But the assumption of "role-rationality" has proven to be effective in terms of portraying the bulk of the behavior of large numbers of consumers. It is assumed that for the political consumer or the member, as we have called him, the assumption of "role-rationality" will perform equally well. The second condition requires that there be some method of identifying the empirical referents of the role occupant's benefits and costs. Much of this chapter is devoted to the specification of these referents.

Finally, we assume that individuals have access to a good deal of information in evaluating their alternatives. They are able to perceive the utility functions of other members of the social structure, and they are aware of the actions taken by others in the past. We assume, however, that individuals do not possess information that would allow them to calculate with certainty the probabilities other individuals attach to the receipt of benefits from their alternatives. Whenever the behavior of individuals is contingent upon these estimated probabilities, therefore, our information condition makes it impossible for anyone to predict the behavior of others with certainty.[22]

---

[22] This information condition is a highly specific one. We believe that our model could be derived for other conditions of imperfect information without altering the thrust of the argument in any fundamental way. In this book, however, we thought it best to develop the model on the basis of an exact assumption about information so that the manipulation of information conditions can be undertaken self-consciously in later works.

Collective Goods

Next, we assume that there are some goods such that if one individual receives them, other individuals will also receive them. Any good exhibiting this characteristic we define as a *collective good*.[23] The set of individuals who receive a collective good constitutes a social structure. The membership of a social structure will consist of n individuals $(a_1, a_2, \ldots, a_n)$. In this book we assume that all collective goods are received by the same set of individuals. That is, any social structure defined by additional collective goods will be assumed to be co-extensive with the social structure defined by the first collective good. In addition, we assume that only members of the social structure contribute to the supply of any given collective good. As a result, this book contains a model of "closed" social structures, which are fully isolated from other social structures. Since an analysis of the interactions among social structures would seriously complicate the initial formulation of our model, we have chosen to leave this set of questions for future extensions of the model.

For the purposes of our derivations we deal only with cases of pure collective goods and do not concern ourselves with possible imperfections or "mixed goods."[24]

---

[23] This definition of collective goods follows that set forth in Olson, *op.cit.*, 13–14.

[24] A number of articles have been written on the empirical relevance of the pure collective good as an ideal type. The argument was touched off by the innovating articles by Paul Samuelson in the *Review of Economics and Statistics:* "The Pure Theory of Public Expenditure," *op. cit.;* "Diagrammatic Exposition of a Theory of Public Expenditure" Nov. 1955, 350–356; and "Aspects of Public Expenditure Theory" Nov. 1958, 332–338. Samuelson's formulation of the problem was attacked as empirically uninteresting by Julius Margolis in an article in the same

It should be pointed out, however, that the collective nature of any good is not an intrinsic characteristic of the good. Rather, it is a function of the market mechanisms of the social structure. Thus, for example, the signals from a lighthouse are often a collective good. If the lighthouse sends signals, any ship can receive them. But imagine a "lighthouse" that sent signals which could be picked up only by special instruments, or which required a decoding device for proper interpretation. Then exclusion would be possible, and the "signals" from the lighthouse would be a collective good only for those ships equipped with the relevant decoding device or special instruments.[25] Although we will refer to situations of this kind from time to time, we offer no formal analysis of such cases in the present book.

Finally, we assume that the individual's demand curve for any given collective good is similar to his demand curve for a private good. Thus, after some point the

---

Review: "A Comment on the Pure Theory of Public Expenditure" Nov. 1955, 347–349. A good summary of the issues at stake is contained in John G. Head's article, "Public Goods and Public Policy," *Public Finance* 17 (1967), 197–219. In addition to the notion of nonexcludability, Head also discusses a second characteristic of Samuelson's "public goods": the consumption of the good by more people does not affect the quality of the good available to each of them. Although this was a second characteristic of public goods as defined by Samuelson, Head has shown that it is not a necessary assumption for most of the conclusions made by Samuelson. Olson's formulation of the problem, in *The Logic of Collective Action,* as well as ours, is based on the assumption of nonexcludability. Our formulation of the model in this book, however, assumes a constant group size.

[25] On this point consult Olson, *op.cit.,* 14, and Kenneth J. Arrow, *Political and Economic Evaluation of Social Effects and Externalities* (mimeographed 1968).

individual receives decreasing marginal utility from the consumption of additional units of any given collective good. That is, the more the individual has already consumed, the less he values the receipt of an additional unit of the same collective good.

Donations for Collective Goods

Consider now the behavior of any individual, a_j, with respect to the donations, $D_j(X_i)$, he will be willing to make toward the supply of some collective good. If $U_j(X_i)$ is a_j's utility valuation of X_i and $P_j(X_i)$ is a_j's estimation of the probability that X_i will be supplied, then a_j's expected value from X_i is $U_j(X_i)P_j(X_i)$. And a_j will evaluate the efficacy of any donation he may make in terms of the net increase he can expect such a donation to produce in his total expected utility. Algebraically, his utility equation for the collective good can be written as:

$$U_j = U_j(X_i)P_j(X_i) - D_j(X_i) \qquad (1.1)$$

It is possible to express mathematically the conditions that will determine the size of any individual's voluntary donations for the provision of the good.[26] He will continue to donate as long as the utility he

[26] From this point onward we will, at times, be concerned with manipulating the mathematical expressions to obtain the conditions governing the individual's decisions. In particular, we will be interested in the effects that the member may bring about by incremental changes in his contributions. We will denote an incremental change in a variable "U" as "dU": a variable preceded by a "d" indicates an infinitesimal increment of that variable. Often we will be interested in the rate of change of one variable or expression as a function of a change in a second variable. This can be expressed as a ratio, referred to in calculus as a "derivative." This fraction consists of a numerator which is an infinitesimal change in the dependent variable and a denominator which is an infinitesimal change in the independent vari-

gets from additional donations is greater than zero: $\dfrac{dU_j}{dD_j(X_i)} > 0$. The utility he receives from his donations

---

able. Thus, $\dfrac{dU}{dD}$ is the rate of change of U as a function of D.

In a situation in which an actor is attempting to maximize one variable, say utility, U, as a function of donations, D, he will continue adding increments of D so long as it brings increments of U sufficient to make $\dfrac{dU}{dD}$ greater than zero. The point at which utility is a maximum as a function of D will have the property that $\dfrac{dU}{dD} = 0$.

Often we will be concerned with obtaining the maxima of expressions containing the sum and products of variables. For those cases, the following two rules governing derivatives in calculus will be of importance:

First, the derivative of a product $U \cdot P$ is equal to the derivative of U times P plus U times the derivative of P.

Algebraically: $\qquad \dfrac{d(U \cdot P)}{dD} = \dfrac{dU}{dD}P + U\dfrac{dP}{dD}.$

Second, the derivative of the sum of U and P is equal to the derivative of U plus the derivative of P.

Algebraically: $\qquad \dfrac{d(U + P)}{dD} = \dfrac{dU}{dD} + \dfrac{dP}{dD}.$

Thus, the maximization of an expression $U \cdot P - D$ as a function of D requires that:

$$\dfrac{d(U \cdot P - D)}{dD} = 0, \text{ or } \dfrac{dU}{dD}P + U\dfrac{dP}{dD} - \dfrac{dD}{dD} = 0.$$

Finally, it should be noted that the analysis which uses differential calculus requires a continuous transformation function between utility and probability, on the one hand, and donations, on the other, if these operations are to be performed. This assumption of continuity is discussed in Chapter Four, where it is shown that the introduction of an agreed-upon decision rule produces a discontinuous transformation function.

33

will stem from: (1) utility increases steming from increases in the probability that the collective good will be supplied, $\dfrac{dP_j(X_i)}{dD_j(X_i)} U_j(X_i)$, and/or (2) utility increases stemming from increases in the amount of the collective good provided, $\dfrac{dU_j(X_i)}{dD_j(X_i)} P_j(X_i)$. These factors can be summarized in one expression that stipulates the conditions that must hold if the individual is to continue to donate:[27]

$$\frac{dU_j}{dD_j(X_i)} = \frac{dU_j(X_i)}{dD_j(X_i)} P_j(X_i)$$
$$+ \frac{dP_j(X_i)}{dD_j(X_i)} U_j(X_i) - 1 > 0 \qquad (1.2)$$

Note, however, that all the terms in the last expression are subject to the effects of strategic interaction among the members of the social structure.[28] This is so because $P_j(X_i)$ is a function of a_j's expectations about the behavior of others. In general, therefore, any individual's total donations will be a function of strategic interactions and cannot be specified exactly through straightforward analysis. It is apparent, nevertheless, that some donations might be given to any individual who promised to set up a collection organization and supply the collective good to the group. The size of these potential donations would be determined by an aggregation of equations like 1.2 and would not necessarily depend on the presence of private-good incentives.

[27] It is important to point out here that the treatment of the second-order maximum conditions has been omitted throughout this book for the sake of brevity of exposition.

[28] Recall that strategic interaction refers to the behavior of two or more individuals whenever the choices of each are contingent upon his estimation of the choices of the other(s). A fuller discussion of such interactions can be found in Chapter Five.

Any individual might perceive this potential for donations and estimate that the resources he could collect along these lines would more than offset the total costs of setting up a collection organization and supplying the collective good. The calculations of such an individual would depend on his estimations of the probable contributions of others. If he expected that the resources he could collect would more than offset his costs, he could promise to supply the good, establish a collection organization, provide the good, and keep the surplus.[29] And everyone would be better off in terms of their utility valuations than they were before such actions were taken.[30]

Let us call such an organizer A and the utility he derives from his activities $U_A(L_A)$. In formal terms, then, the organizer would make his decisions in terms

[29] The innovative behavior of such an individual would be similar to that discussed in Joseph A. Schumpeter, *The Theory of Economic Development* (Cambridge 1934). It should be noted, however, that our innovator, in contrast to the economic entrepreneur analyzed by Schumpeter, is supplying collective goods outside of a market mechanism. We should also note that collective goods will not always be supplied by innovating individuals.

[30] If some individual placed a negative valuation on the collective good, however, he would not be better off even though he donated nothing. In general, any groups of individuals whose expectations about a collective good can be coordinated in such a way that donations can be collected from them in excess of the cost of supply are likely to have their demands met. This is so even if the achievement of these demands would be negatively valued by large numbers of individuals who were not able to coordinate their behavior. A situation of this kind, however, is apt to produce a perfect opportunity for the emergence of an opposition leader, along the lines discussed in Chapter Three. We wish to thank Ronald Brey for drawing our attention to this possibility.

35

of the following expression:

$$U_A(L_A) = U_A(X_A) + \sum_{j=1}^{n} D_j(A) - C(X_A) - C(O_A) \qquad (1.3)$$

where $U_A(X_A)$ is the prospective leader's own valuation of the collective goods he promises to supply; $\sum_{j=1}^{n} D_j(A)$ is the sum of the donations that the leader can collect; $C(X_A)$ is the cost of supplying the goods; and $C(O_A)$ is the cost of the collection organization. When an individual perceives this expression to be positive, he will undertake the actions involved in organizing the group.[31] That is, when he perceives that he can gain more from providing the good than his efforts cost, he will organize the group. Any individual who undertakes these actions we will call a *political leader* or a *political entrepreneur*.[32]

Contracts

So far, the only contributions the leader receives are based on the members' expectations that their donations

[31] This is only true under the assumption that his opportunity costs for such actions are zero. Here, we make this assumption to minimize the complexity of the argument. It can be relaxed, however, without vitally affecting the propositions derived in subsequent sections.

[32] In the case where a political leader already exists, our original description of the behavior of individual members of the social structure must be formulated somewhat differently. Here donations will be made to a leader already in office, and the collective goods will be those supplied by this leader. Thus, equation 1.1 can be rewritten as:

$$U_j(L_A) = U_j(X_A)P_j(X_A) - D_j(A) \qquad (1.4)$$

And equation 1.2 can be rewritten as:

$$\frac{dU_j(L_A)}{dD_j(A)} = \frac{dU_j(X_A)}{dD_j(A)} P_j(X_A) + \frac{dP_j(X_A)}{dD_j(A)} U_j(X_A) - 1 > 0 \qquad (1.5)$$

will be effective in increasing the probability or quantity of supply of the collective good. Equation 1.3, however, indicates that the leader must gather the resources from which he hopes both to fashion a collection organization and to supply the collective good. Some of these resources must be private goods, and what is cost to the leader may become income for someone else. Therefore, the leader controls potential private-good incentives through which he can attempt to increase contributions.

From the perspective of the ordinary members, $C(O_A)$ and $C(X_A)$ are potential "contracts." If, for the sake of simplicity of exposition, we assume a fixed profit rate in the economy (r), a recipient of such contracts might be willing to offer contributions to get them so long as these contributions were smaller than the expected profits from his contracts. Thus, $r[C(O_A) + C(X_A)]$ would be the maximum contributions the leader could hope to get in exchange for the contracts. The ordinary member, however, would be willing to contribute on this basis only insofar as such contributions help him to gain additional profits from contracts. This can happen if the member is able to increase his share of the contracts, $f_j(A)$, or if there is an increase in the total size of the leader's contracts, $C(O_A) + C(X_A)$. Under these conditions, the individual member will continue to contribute as long as he receives a positive return.

What conditions determine whether the individual member will find it profitable to contribute to the leader in order to acquire contracts? The most obvious condition is a division of labor in the social structure such that the services of different individuals are required for the production of different goods. In such cases, the value to the individual member of having a particular collective good supplied will be the utility he gets from

37

the consumption of the good plus the profits he expects to receive if his services are employed in producing the good. As a result, we would expect that the greater the division of labor in the social structure, the larger the proportion of contributions that will stem from the desire of the members to increase their share of the contracts let by the leader. Moreover, whenever substitute collective goods being considered for inclusion in the leader's program require different factors of production, we would expect the owners of factors of production to compete for the adoption of a program utilizing their factors through contributions to the leader.

From the perspective of the individual member, contracts and contributions for contracts must be added to the equation governing his relationship with the leader. Contributions of this kind are distinguishable from donations because they arise from different motivations on the part of the members. In specifying the resultant utility function of the ordinary member, however, we find it convenient to combine them into one formula. If contributions for contracts are treated as donations algebraically, the utility a_j derives from his membership in the social structure when A is the leader can be expressed as:

$$U_j(L_A) = U_j(X_A)P_j(X_A) \\ + f_j(A)r[C(X_A) + C(O_A)] - D_j(A) \qquad (1.6)$$

And the total contributions that the utility-maximizing member will make to the leader will be governed by the marginal condition that he will stop donating when $\dfrac{dU_j(L_A)}{dD_j(A)} = 0$. In other words, he will continue to contribute so long as the expected benefit from his added contribution is greater than the cost of that added bit of contribution. These conditions can be derived in the same fashion as those stated in equations 1.2 and 1.5.[33] Any such donations will be reflected in the revenue term, $\sum_{j=1}^{n} D_j(L_A)$, in the leader's role premise.

Private-Good Incentives—The General Case

Contracts are not the only positive, private-good incentive the leader can manipulate. In fact, a leader may be able to supply private goods—to some or all of the members—which they value more than the cost of production. If this is the case, the leader can "sell" the goods at a profit. Activities of this kind would increase the profitability of occupying the leadership role. Any political leader who acts in terms of these considerations is acting as a classical economic entrepreneur, and his behavior is subject to traditional economic analysis. Although a leader may well have a competitive advantage in the provision of some private goods due to the externalities of his political leadership role, it is possible that the added revenue obtained through the use of private-good incentives will cut down the size of the voluntary donations he receives. Members of the group, seeing that the leader has an alternate source of revenue, may well decide that their donations are not as essential as they had previously believed. Thus, the introduction of

[33] Specifically, the marginal conditions for the contributions that the individual makes in order to maximize his utility are now:

$$\frac{dU_j(L_A)}{dD_j(A)} = \frac{dU_j(X_A)}{dD_j(A)} P_j(X_A) + \frac{dP_j(X_A)}{dD_j(A)} U_j(X_A)$$
$$+ r\left([C(O_A) + C(X_A)] \frac{df_j(A)}{dD_j(A)} + f_j(A) \frac{d[C(O_A) + C(X_A)]}{dD_j(A)}\right)$$
$$- 1 > 0 \qquad (1.7)$$

See note 26 for an explanation of the steps in this derivation.

39

private-good incentives along this line will not guarantee an increase in the leader's net revenue.[34]

We will not incorporate these considerations into our formal model at this stage, reserving further comment on their implications for the following chapter.

Coercion and Revenues

So far two distinct sources of revenue for the political leader have been identified: donations, and exchanges involving positively valued private goods. There are, however, alternative ways for the political leader to obtain resources. In the first instance, he may impose a tax on some or all of the members of the social structure.

We define a tax as a contribution that an individual makes to avoid a sanction that he expects to be imposed on him if he fails to make the specified contribution.[35] Individuals will make such contributions only if the expected cost of not making them is greater than the value of the tax being collected. That is, the individual will pay those taxes that he is forced to pay.[36] To obtain tax revenues, therefore, the leader's collection organiza-

[34] Although Olson devotes considerable space to an analysis of the effects of private-good incentives on the supply of collective goods, he does not mention this possible effect. This omission is a consequence of the fact that he felt that no voluntary contributions for the supply of collective goods would be forthcoming.

[35] In this essay, we define a sanction as the imposition of a distinct, negatively valued good on an individual. Thus, the act of discontinuing an individual's supply of a positively valued good does not constitute a sanction by our definition. Note, however, that sanctions can be either collective or private goods.

[36] It is true, however, that some individuals may make donations over and above any taxes they pay. But in a noncompetitive situation, the higher the taxes, the fewer the donations (as distinct from contributions for contracts) a political leader will receive.

40

tion must be capable of inflicting punishment that is more costly to the individual than the payment of the tax itself. If, for example, the leader presented a_j with a tax bill that was greater than the sanctions his organization could impose on a_j, a_j would choose to accept the sanctions rather than pay the taxes. Thus, the taxes a leader can collect in any given time period are a function of the coercive potential of his collection organization.

Assuming that the members of the social structure may have to pay taxes, we can restate the utility function of the individual member. If the taxes a_j pays to the leader A are designated as $T_j(A)$, the utility function of a_j then becomes:

$$U_j(L_A) = U_j(X_A)P_j(X_A) + f_j(A) r[C(O_A) + C(X_A)] \\ - D_j(A) - T_j(A) \qquad (1.8)$$

Similarly, the possibility of tax revenue must be incorporated into the utility function of the political leader. His utility function then becomes:

$$U_A(L_A) = U_A(X_A) + \sum_{j=1}^{n} D_j(A) + \sum_{j=1}^{n} T_j(A) \\ - [C(O_A) + C(X_A)] \qquad (1.9)$$

Note that a tax is a contribution made by an individual to avoid a sanction that he expects to be imposed directly on *him* if *he* does not make a contribution. Fundamental to the notion of taxation, therefore, is the ability of the leader to direct sanctions at specified individuals. But there is another way in which a political leader can employ sanctions to obtain resources. He can threaten an entire group, as a group, through some procedure such as threatening to impose random sanctions if a certain volume of contributions is not forthcoming from the group as a whole. Under these conditions, indi-

41

viduals would make contributions for collective goods. That is, the avoidance of random sanctions would be a collective good for the group as a whole. We will refer to any contributions a leader obtains by this method as *extorted revenue* or *extortions*.[37]

Personality and Revenues

So far we have dealt only with revenues contributed to the leader by the members of the social structure.[38] Leaders may, however, receive revenue that is not contributed by the members of the social structure. We have already tacitly included one source of revenue of this type: the utility the leader himself receives from the collective good he supplies, $U_A(X_A)$. But the leader may

[37] Under certain conditions, extortion may become a major source of revenue for a political leader. Guerrilla warfare tactics based on random terror, for example, can be explained in these terms. To avoid an unnecessary complication of the utility functions of the leader and the members of the group, however, we will absorb extortions into the term representing taxation. When we discuss taxation in subsequent sections and use the term $T_j(A)$, therefore, we will be referring to extortions as well. Nevertheless, the distinction between the two types of revenue can be reintroduced whenever it is required for specific arguments in later sections.

[38] The reader may find it helpful in following the analysis of subsequent sections to group the four sources of contributed revenue to allow two dimensions. First, there is a distinction between contributions made to avoid the imposition of sanctions (i.e. taxes and extortions) and contributions made in exchange for some positive improvement in the welfare of the contributor (i.e. donations and purchases of private goods). Second, it is useful to distinguish between contributions made to affect the supply of collective goods (i.e. donations and extortions) and contributions made to affect the supply of private goods (i.e. purchases and taxes). All these types of contributions (or sources of revenue from the perspective of the leader) can be sum-

42

have additional sources of noncontributed revenue. We have assumed prior to this point that the cost of a collection organization and the cost of supplying collective goods are pure costs to the political leader, since both operations require the expenditure of resources. It is not unreasonable to assume, however, that a leader might derive some pleasure (utility) simply from being the head of the administrative apparatus required to make collections and supply collective goods. For simplicity of exposition, let us assume that the pleasure any individual leader derives from this administrative function is linearly proportional to the size of the apparatus.[39] The proportionality constant for the revenue that a leader, A, receives from this source, then, can be represented as b_A. And we can say that the leader, A, gets the following utility from presiding over the collection organization and the supply of collective goods: $b_A[C(O_A) + C(X_A)]$. We will assume that the size of the proportionality constant for this source of revenue can differ from leader to leader and that its size will be a function of personality in individual cases.

If we incorporate this modification of the leader's costs

---

marized in the following two-by-two matrix.

SOURCES AND TYPES OF CONTRIBUTIONS

	NEGATIVE SANCTIONS	POSITIVE INDUCEMENTS
COLLECTIVE GOODS	Extortions	Donations
PRIVATE GOODS	Taxes	Purchases

[39] If we hold questions of efficiency in abeyance, the cost of the administrative apparatus may be used as a rough measure of its size.

43

into equation 1.9, we obtain the complete equation in terms of which a political leader evaluates his role:

$$U_A(L_A) = U_A(X_A) + \sum_{j=1}^{n} D_j(A) + \sum_{j=1}^{n} T_j(A) \\ - (1 - b_A)[C(O_A) + C(X_A)] \quad (1.10)$$

The role premise of the leader for situations in which there is no competition for the occupancy of his role, therefore, will consist of the maximization of this expression. He will, in other words, attempt to obtain the maximum utility difference between his revenues and costs from his role.

The introduction of this modification into the role premise of the leader does not alter the form of the role premise of the ordinary member of the social structure. For the sake of completeness, however, let us restate the equation defining the role premise of the ordinary member for noncompetitive situations:

$$U_j(L_A) = U_j(X_A)P_j(X_A) + f_j(A)\,r[C(O_A) + C(X_A)] \\ - D_j(A) - T_j(A) \quad (1.11)$$

The ordinary member, like the leader, will attempt to obtain the maximum utility surplus from activities conducted in terms of his role.

CHAPTER TWO

The Consequences of
Noncompetitive Politics

IT IS NOW POSSIBLE TO
utilize the model formulated in Chapter One to derive
a number of hypotheses about politics in noncompetitive
situations.

THE EFFECTS OF PERSONALITY DIFFERENCES
AMONG LEADERS

Personality differences may be important in explaining
the behavior of political leaders. In the model, such
differences are reflected in the b term which was introduced, but not fully discussed, in the previous chapter.[1]
At the simplest level, this term modifies the costs to a
leader, A, of providing a collection organization and
supplying collective goods.[2] Thus, without the b_A term,

---

[1] As noted on pp. 42–44, a political leader may derive utility
simply from presiding over the administrative apparatus associated with his role. It has been assumed that the utility obtained
in this fashion is proportional to the total cost of the apparatus
and that the resultant proportionality constant, b, is fixed for
any given individual. Thus, the utility a leader, A, derives from
this source can be designated as $b_A[C(O_A) + C(X_A)]$.

[2] It is possible that individual leaders will have different personal preferences regarding various aspects of the administrative
apparatus from which they obtain utility. Some leaders, for

the cost of the collection organization and the collective goods is:

$$[C(O_A) + C(X_A)] \tag{2.1}$$

The introduction of the b_A term, however, changes this cost function. The net cost of the collection organization and the collective goods now becomes:

$$(1 - b_A)[C(O_A) + C(X_A)] \tag{2.2}$$

The Behavioral Consequences of the b Term

Compare leaders who have a $b > O$ with those who have a $b < O$. The first type of leader can be called an "eager leader" since he will accept leadership positions even when his other revenues do not cover the costs of organization and supplying the collective goods. In extreme cases, a political leader of this type will pay substantial sums for the privilege of occupying the leader's position in his social structure. Compare this case to the "reluctant leader," whose b term is negative. Such an individual may have to receive a subsidy, above and beyond the leader's normal surplus, to accept the leadership role at all.

Any leader with a high positive b will have a comparative advantage whenever there is competition for the leadership role; such leaders require smaller (or even negative) contributions for any given size of leader's surplus and can therefore supply collective goods to the members of the social structure on a more efficient basis. In this sense, it may be said that an individual with a

example, may get more utility from the coercive aspect of the apparatus, while others may be particularly interested in its collective-good aspect. In this book, the differences that occur at this level of generality are not analyzed. Rather, we will focus on the overall utility any given leader derives from the b term.

high positive b pursues the role of political leader largely "for its own sake." The rewards he gets from simply holding the office constitute a major factor in his valuation of the role. In contrast, the leader with a low (or negative) b will be more strongly motivated to engage in activities not directly associated with the administrative aspects of his role. It follows from this analysis that in social structures where there is competition for the leadership roles, those aspiring leaders with the highest positive b terms will have a competitive advantage and will gain control of a disproportionate number of these roles.[3]

The Fanatical Leader

It is also possible to analyze the consequences of having a leader who is characterized by a b term greater than 1. Any such leader would find it worthwhile to specialize in setting up collection organizations or supplying collective goods. He would make a "profit" of $b_A - 1$ for every dollar he spent on collection organizations or the supply of collective goods, and it would be rational for him to increase his expenditures on these items continuously. He would continue to act in this fashion until the cost of collecting the resources he was expending on collection organizations or collective goods fully offset the profit he was obtaining by supplying them (i.e., until the marginal dollar he could collect in revenue cost him $b_A - 1$ to collect). Any such leader who decided to specialize in the supply of collective goods could be described as a populist demagogue. In effect, he

[3] See also William Riker, *The Theory of Political Coalitions* (New Haven 1962). Riker discusses some of the implications of a leader's valuing his office for its own sake. His notion of the bankruptcy of leadership would appear to be relevant to our discussion at this point.

47

would "exploit" the members of the social structure in order to supply them with collective goods from which he could obtain a "profit." From the perspective of the members, the result would be a superoptimal supply of collective goods.

THE QUALITY OF LEADERSHIP

In the previous chapter, it was argued that no individual would assume the role of political leader if he could not obtain a surplus from this action. Even if there is a readily identifiable surplus, however, there may be no individual who wishes to occupy the role of political leader since the occupancy of this role may involve opportunity costs. For an individual to desire to occupy the role of political leader, therefore, he must believe that the potential profit associated with this role will be greater than the rewards for alternative activities. This consideration has several consequences affecting the quality of leadership in any social structure.

Let us define the "public sector" of a social structure in terms of those goods supplied through organizations set up by political leaders[4] and assume that the size of the leader's surplus increases (though not necessarily in a linear fashion) as the size of the public sector increases. Under these conditions, the greater the size of the public sector, relative to the rest of the economy, the lower will be the opportunity costs of occupying the role of political leader. As a consequence, the larger the size of the public sector, the greater will be the segment of the social structure from which individuals will

[4] The size of the public sector might be calculated in terms of any of several indicators. The value of all the contracts distributed by the leader, the size of the leader's tax revenues, or some combination of the two might serve as indicators.

48

find it worthwhile to compete for the leadership role. The quality of leadership would then rise with the growth of the public sector.

The same line of argument suggests that if the rate of growth of the public sector fails to keep pace with the rate of growth of the overall economy, leadership recruitment will be increasingly confined to the lower-income strata of the society.[5] In extreme cases, it may be worth no one's while to become a political leader, with the result that leadership recruitment can only be accomplished through some such mechanism as a lottery.[6] Conversely, if (as is often argued) economic development is accompanied by an increase in the size of the public sector relative to the private sector, competition for political leadership roles will tend to become more broadly based as a society undergoes the process of modernization.[7]

The Leader's Mix of Revenues

This section contains an analysis of a number of options open to the political leader in manipulating his contributed revenues in the interests of maximizing his surplus. These options may not always be independent

[5] This phenomenon is illustrated by the recruitment of leaders into the big-city political machines that flourished in the United States around the turn of the century. In that case, the public sector was relatively small, and political leaders were recruited from the lower-income strata of the society.

[6] This may explain the recruitment of leaders for some political roles through a lottery mechanism in some of the ancient Greek city states.

[7] Interesting illustrations of the relationships mentioned in this section can be found in Merle Kling, "Towards a Theory of Power and Political Instability in Latin America," *The Western Political Quarterly* 9 (March 1956), 21–35.

of questions concerning noncontributed revenues. But for purposes of discussion, assume that the leader's revenues from the $U(X_i)$ and b terms are of a fixed form for any given leader and, therefore, not subject to manipulation.

Efficiency Issues

A political leader has considerable leeway to manipulate the components of his contributed revenue. He can substitute taxes for donations, sell positively valued private goods rather than collect taxes, and otherwise specify the forms of contributions he will receive from the members of his social structure. How does the leader arrive at decisions concerning such matters? In analyzing this question, we will assume that the only sources of revenue the leader can tap are donations and taxes. This assumption can later be relaxed in order to consider exchanges involving positively valued private goods as a source of revenue for the leader.

In choosing a mix of donations and taxes which will maximize his surplus, a leader must consider two sets of factors. First, he must take into account the strategic interdependencies between donations and taxes. Second, he must think about the differences in organizational costs which arise from combining various procedures for raising revenues and supplying collective goods.

It is easy to demonstrate the relevance of strategic behavior to the leader's problem of selecting an optimal mix between donations and taxes but difficult to specify the precise impact of such behavior. Ordinary members of a social structure donate resources to the leader on a voluntary basis whenever such donations have a positive effect on their expected value for a given collective good. By introducing taxes as another source of revenue, however, the leader runs a risk that many donors will reduce the size of their donations. Individual members may act in this fashion either (1) because they no longer feel their donations are required to insure the supply of the collective goods in question or (2) because they feel that the efficiency with which the collective good was supplied will be reduced as the leader diverts resources to the development of a coercive apparatus to insure that taxes are collected. But how much will donations fall off for any given increase in the tax rate? This is clearly a critical question for a rational political leader, but it is difficult to answer precisely since it opens up the whole problem of strategic interaction. The members of a social structure may well try to persuade the leader that any increase in taxes will be more than offset by the resultant drop in donations, while the leader will attempt to persuade the members that the new taxes should not lead to a reduction in donations since they will not be employed as a substitute for the donations. The outcome of such an interaction will be the result of a bargaining process and may well vary with such things as the past history of the relationship[8] and the level of taxes at the time of the interaction.

Strategic considerations are not, however, the only factors the rational leader will have to consider in selecting an optimal mix of revenues from donations and taxes. In fact, the leader will be faced with a series of efficiency questions since the agencies required to collect taxes are apt to differ from those needed to gather donations and since some arrangements for the supply of collective goods will be less costly than others. Under the circumstances, the leader will have to consider which

[8] The history of the relationship is likely to be important since it will generate precedents that influence the estimations of individuals about the probable actions of others in future time periods.

51

of his alternative mixes of revenues is most efficient given the collection organizations required and the nature of the collective goods to be supplied.

One type of efficiency calculation arises from the issue of scale, or the effect of the size of an existing organization on the cost of supplying additional units of a good through the same organization. In some cases, the cost of supplying an additional unit of the good through an expansion of production will be less than the cost of producing the last unit of the good. Such a situation is commonly described in terms of the notion of decreasing marginal costs. When the cost of an additional unit of the good is more than the cost of the last unit, on the other hand, a situation involving increasing marginal costs arises. In general, the rational political leader will take into account any such changes in costs arising from the scale of his operations.

The influence of effects of scale is especially clear in the case of donations for the supply of collective goods. Within any specified group, there will always be a distinct upper limit to the amount of donations a leader can collect for any given collective good. This upper limit will be set by the aggregate utility the members of the group could derive from the good in question. Moreover, there are two reasons why this upper limit is unlikely to be reached in real-world situations. First, there is the impact of transaction costs. That is, it may cost the leader more to collect some of the potential donations than they are worth to him. Second, even when transaction costs are negligible, there are likely to be strategic interactions among the members of the group and between the members and the leader in which each member will attempt to manipulate the size of his donations to his own advantage. In some cases, the leader will be able to minimize the loss of donations through this process by manipulating the members' information about costs, various probabilities, and the actual supply of the collective good. But even so, such actions on the part of the leader will be circumscribed by the upper limit on donations which he cannot manipulate. Other things being equal, therefore, it follows that the political leader will eventually face a situation involving serious diseconomies of scale in connection with additional expenditures on organizational arrangements designed to collect donations.

In the cases of taxes, the political leader may have considerably more leeway to collect revenue, even though he will ultimately face an upper limit in this area as well. The upper limit on taxation is the ability of the members of the social structure to pay without suffering a reduction in their productivity. Since this upper limit is considerably higher than the aggregate valuation the members are apt to place on any given set of collective goods, decreasing returns may not begin to occur as soon in the case of taxes as in the case of donations. On the contrary, it may well happen that the leader can obtain substantial economies in the collection of taxes. That is, the larger the apparatus for the collection of taxes, the cheaper it may become for the leader to collect each additional unit of taxes. Under these conditions, the leader is likely to find taxation a highly attractive source of revenue. And the limitations on his ability to tax the members of his social structure are apt to arise from extrinsic factors such as political competition, rather than from problems of efficiency in the collection of taxes.

Questions of scale, however, are not the only efficiency issues that the rational political leader must take into account. A second type of efficiency issue may arise from the emergence of externalities or complementarities asso-

53

ciated with the organizational arrangements set up for the collection of various types of revenue and the production of different collective goods.[9] Thus, an organization set up to collect one type of revenue may increase the leader's efficiency in collecting other forms of revenue or supplying different collective goods. Analogously, the apparatus required to supply a particular collective good may increase the leader's efficiency in supplying additional collective goods or collecting new forms of revenue. It is likely to happen, for example, that the organization a leader establishes to collect donations will be useful in collecting taxes as well. In such circumstances, the leader may be able to derive significant savings if he supplements his revenue from donations by collecting taxes.

Under these conditions, the leader's decisions concerning his collection organization and the supply of collective goods will usually be interdependent. If he supplies "law and order" as a collective good, for example, he will generally need a coercive organization, and such an organization would often be capable of extracting taxes efficiently. Conversely, even if the leader does not begin with the objective of supplying law and order, he may find himself in possession of an organization with sufficient taxing power to make it profitable for him to go into the business of supplying law and order. Such organizational complementarities will often account for the propensity of political entrepreneurs toward

[9] An externality is a by-product of some action undertaken for other purposes, the value of which is not taken into account by a market mechanism. Externalities can be either negative or positive. A complementarity is an interdependence between two activities such that the occurrence or presence of one facilitates any effort to undertake the other. Some complementarities are likely to be externalities.

54

diversification in the supply of collective goods and in their sources of revenue.[10]

The relationship between diversification in the supply of collective goods and the revenues that a leader collects can be examined most simply in the case of a leader who collects only donations. Such a leader will be faced eventually with a declining demand curve for any specific collective good he supplies and, therefore, with decreasing marginal returns from the supply of additional quantities of the good. Thus, he will find it worth his while at some point to diversify into the supply of other collective goods to expand his surplus. And such considerations will remain important so long as donations continue to form a part of the leader's revenue, even without the introduction of extrinsic pressures for the supply of additional collective goods.

In addition, a political leader who depends upon donations will be wary of collective goods that are durable or have high initial costs of supply. Durable collective goods raise problems for such a leader since they limit his activities to a "one-shot" enterprise. If he has promised to provide bridges, for example, and the bridges are supplied, the leader must turn to new programs or vacate the leadership role. Collective goods with high initial costs likewise pose problems for the leader. They will involve difficult problems of coordinating expectations to give people a sense of efficacy and, therefore, an incentive to contribute. A leader contemplating a program involving the supply of a collective good with a high initial cost who does not have a secure

---

[10] A particularly striking study of the relationship between types of revenue and collective goods supplied can be found in Karl Wittvogel, *Oriental Despotism* (New Haven 1957), esp. 1–100.

hold of his office on a long-term basis will therefore consider such a venture very risky indeed. Thus, non-durables and goods with smooth supply functions will be attractive both because they offer continuity of profitable action to the leader and because they represent less risky ventures.

Efficiency Calculations and Private Goods

Revenue derived from the sale of positively valued private goods may interact negatively with the donations that a leader can collect just as taxation does. Members of the social structure who know about the new source of revenue, for example, are apt to have a lower incentive to donate to the leader on a voluntary basis since they will feel that their donations are less critical to the leader's efforts to supply the collective goods in question.[11] Once again, however, the exact amount of the resultant reductions in donations will be determined on the basis of strategic behavior.

Revenue derived from the sale of private goods, like revenue from donations, will have a distinct upper limit. Thus, for example, a leader cannot conceivably receive more in contributions for contracts than the profits that the members of his group derive from the contracts. Nevertheless, a political leader may have special incentives to provide private goods other than contracts. Thus, he may find that his activities in supplying collective goods generate externalities that make it profitable for him to supply the members with such private goods. His organization, for example, may give him an

---

[11] Note that this interaction only takes place if the members have information regarding the leader's revenue and cost functions.

advantage either in the manufacture or in the distribution of a particular private good.[12] This will be especially likely if he can employ coercion to achieve this result. In this connection, the political leader may be able to use coercion to monopolize the supply of a private good, thereby putting himself in a position to reap a monopolist's profits. To the extent that any of these conditions holds, the leader will find it worthwhile to supply positively valued private goods to supplement the income he receives from the provision of collective goods. The profitability of such activities on the part of a political leader can be analyzed through the use of classical economic theory.

DIFFERENCES BETWEEN POLITICAL AND ECONOMIC ENTREPRENEURS

There are both similarities and differences between economic entrepreneurs and political entrepreneurs. At the most general level, an entrepreneur can be defined as an individual who seeks to make a profit from the supply of some good to the members of a group. Economists view entrepreneurs as individuals who are concerned with the supply of private goods for a profit. We conceptualize a political entrepreneur as an individual who seeks to make a profit by supplying collective goods. As such, it seems clear that these two types of entrepreneur are actually polar subcategories of the general conception of an entrepreneur.

[12] One particularly interesting good that the leader might well find profitable to supply is a prize for a lottery. Especially in cases where the costs of a coercive organization are high and the tax mechanism is approaching the point of diminishing returns, the leader may use his resources to establish a lottery.

Although the two types of entrepreneur are separable for purposes of theoretical analysis, the activities of real-life entrepreneurs are unlikely to fall neatly into one category or the other. As noted in the previous section, there are various conditions under which it is profitable for political entrepreneurs to become economic entrepreneurs by supplying private goods. Similarly, at times economic entrepreneurs may find that their activities involve externalities relating to various collective goods. In such cases, economic entrepreneurs will branch out into the supply of collective goods for a profit, thereby adding to their total income.

Moreover, some of the externalities linking collective and private goods are apt to be associated with the phenomena of scale and returns to scale. As the size of a political entrepreneur's overall operation increases (within a given social structure), there is a growing tendency for him to diversify his activities into the provision of private goods. Although there may be several intervening links between a general argument of this kind and specific cases, such considerations might well be important in explaining the increasing participation of modern governments in the private-good sectors of their respective economies. A parallel argument can also be made concerning the growing emphasis that large-scale economic entrepreneurs place on the provision of collective goods for their employees. Two extreme cases that illustrate these tendencies are the socialist state and the company town.

The principal concern of this book, however, is the role of the political entrepreneur. Just as economists have generally simplified the analysis of the entrepreneur by focusing on the private-good aspects of his behavior, we find it useful to concentrate on the collective-good aspects of his behavior.

COLLECTIVE GOODS AND OPTIMALITY OF SUPPLY

Economists, especially welfare economists, have long been interested in the attainment of optimal equilibria in societies. Any socially optimal equilibrium involves reaching a point on the production possibility frontier (i.e. full employment of resources) for the society as a whole. It also requires that the society be at a most preferred point on the production possibility frontier. This, in turn, implies that the marginal costs of additional units of all goods are shared by the members of the society in exactly the same proportion as the benefits derived from the goods.

In discussing the consequences of introducing the phenomenon of political entrepreneurship into the analysis of socially optimal equilibria, we will assume that the private-good sector of the economy is perfectly competitive (i.e. the marginal conditions necessary for optimality hold for all private goods). Starting with such an assumption, let us introduce the presence of collective goods supplied through the activities of a political entrepreneur. What is the likelihood of achieving a socially optimal equilibrium given the leader's role in the social structure?

Consider a situation in which the political leader relies solely on donations. This case has been analyzed by a number of economists. The basic problem in reaching optimality of supply in such situations is well summarized by Olson as follows:

> The necessary conditions for the optimal provision of a collective good, through the voluntary and independent action of the members of the group, can, however, be stated very simply. The marginal cost of additional units of the collective good must be shared in

exactly the same proportion as the additional benefits. Only if this is done will each member find that his own marginal costs and benefits are equal at the same time that the total marginal cost equals the total or aggregate marginal benefit. If marginal costs are shared in *any* other way, the amount of collective good provided will be sub-optimal.[13]

Given strategic behavior, however, it is extremely unlikely that every member of a group will contribute on a voluntary basis up to the level of his marginal benefit from additional units of the goods in question. A tendency toward suboptimality is therefore strongly indicated whenever the collective good is supplied on the basis of donations.[14]

Another potential source of a leader's revenue, however, is taxation. To be consistent with the achievement of a socially optimal equilibrium, taxes must be levied on a cost-benefit basis. But there are two major barriers to such an ideal solution. First, the members of a group pay taxes on the basis of the coercive potential of the leader. And although it is conceivable that the leader could employ his coercive potential to approximate a cost-benefit schedule of taxation, there is nothing whatsoever in noncompetitive situations which would lead one to expect that such an arrangement would in fact be forthcoming. Second, the leader never participates in a "perfectly competitive industry" with respect to the supply of collective goods. As a result, he will always have the ability to obtain a surplus similar to monopoly profits, a situation that precludes the achievement of an optimal supply of the collective goods.[15]

[13] Olson, *op.cit.*, 30–31.

[14] Baumol, *op.cit.*, Chapter 12.

[15] A more extensive discussion of this point can be found in Chapter Three, pp. 66–72.

This conflict between the interests of the political leader and the requirements of social optimality has been recognized by political analysts at least since the time of Plato. Plato himself saw quite clearly the difficulty in recruiting a leader who would act in the interests of the populace at large. His solution was to insist on the importance of finding a "philosopher king" who would be motivated solely by a desire to take care of the needs of the society as a whole. And in fact only an individual concerned exclusively with the interests of the populace would permit the achievement of a socially optimal equilibrium, thereby foregoing the monopoly profits he could otherwise obtain. Such an individual could not be self-interested.

The introduction of revenues based on the sale of positively valued private goods does nothing to improve the chances of achieving social optimality. If the political leader is to make a profit and finance the supply of collective goods from the sale of private goods, either part of the price for these goods must constitute a form of donations or the markets for them must be imperfect. If the price the leader receives for private goods is higher than the competitive price, the leader is actually receiving a form of disguised donations, and these donations are subject to the analysis outlined at the beginning of this section. Thus, there is no guaranteed social benefit associated with the participation of a political entrepreneur in private-good markets for more than the normal profits.[16] Likewise, if the political entrepreneur is

---

[16] The production and sale of some private goods may have positive externalities with respect to the supply of collective goods. As a result, the cost to the leader of providing certain collective goods may go down, and he may find it profitable to increase their supply. This tendency may be reinforced by any decline in donations which occurs when the members of

61

not faced with a perfect market for private goods, a requisite for the achievement of a socially optimal equilibrium is violated. Thus, the introduction of positively valued private goods as a source of revenue for leaders in no case leads to a movement toward social optimality.

It follows from this discussion that *all* economies will operate on a suboptimal basis: collective goods are always nonoptimally supplied.

EXPLOITATION: THE TENDENCY TOWARD GREAT DIVERGENCE BETWEEN OPTIMAL AND ACTUAL SUPPLY OF COLLECTIVE GOODS

Leaders receive contributions or revenues from the general membership of the group. The collective goods that the leader provides in return may compensate the members for their contributions, but there is no guarantee that this will in fact be the case. To the extent that the leader can employ sanctions to increase his income by supplying fewer collective goods and/or raising taxes, his interests and those of the general membership are antithetical.

The problems the leader faces if he relies on voluntary donations for revenue have already been noted. Not only are such donations subject to the vagaries of strategic interaction among the members, but there is clearly an upper limit to the resources the leader can so command. Thus, he could never obtain more from donations than the area under the aggregate demand curve for the goods

---

the group notice the leader's private-good profit. Though these tendencies might move the supply of collective goods closer to the optimum level, however, there is no reason to believe that these considerations would actually result in the achievement of the optimum. On the contrary, all the other arguments set forth in this section would still hold.

he is to supply. Similarly, the increase in his revenue arising from positively valued private-good exchanges is limited. He can obtain no more than the profit margin on subcontracts, and, in the absence of coercion, he cannot make more than the profit margin on the supply of any private goods he markets.

Coercion, however, overcomes some of these limitations on his income. Taxing through the use of a coercive organization has many advantages from his perspective. If he provides coercion at a fixed level, he can virtually guarantee his income, and he can increase the size of his revenue by increasing the size of his coercive organization. True, there must eventually come a point of diminishing returns, where any increment of coercion will fail to yield a commensurate rise in tax revenue, but this point for taxation is likely to be considerably beyond the analogous point for donations. With coercive taxation the leader is not limited by the shape of the aggregate demand curve for collective goods, as he is in the case of donations for collective goods. In this respect, he is not only in a better position than an economic entrepreneur, he is even in a better position than the monopolist. He can furnish almost any level of collective goods and force the consumers to "buy" them. In the extreme, it can be expected that some leaders will lower the level of the goods they are supplying and raise their taxes at the same time.

Given these advantages of taxation as a means of raising revenue, it is apparent that a rational political entrepreneur will have strong incentives to rely on taxation. There will therefore be a tendency toward raising his income at the members' expense. In this sense, he will become an exploiter.

Even in the absence of competition, however, there are limits to this kind of exploitation. If it is possible

63

for an individual to leave his particular social structure (i.e. give up his membership) at some cost to himself, the leader will be limited in his taxing potential by the level of that cost. If he taxes an individual beyond that level, the individual will prefer to leave the social structure, and the leader will lose the revenue he could have obtained from the individual. The leader could surmount this limitation by acting to raise the costs of leaving the social structure. But such actions would clearly involve additional costs to him and would have to be assessed on the basis of their profitability.[17]

Yet even if the cost to the individual of leaving the social structure is the forefeiture of his life, the leader faces a limit to his potential tax revenue. He may tax a member of the social structure to the subsistence level if he has sufficient coercive potential, but he can go no further if he hopes to maintain his income from that individual over a period of time. The logical extreme of this argument is the case of slavery, where a political entrepreneur acquires total control over his subjects and extracts whatever he pleases from them in exchange for their continued existence.[18]

The reader may object, at this point, that the picture painted is too bleak. The role of the political leaders and the interactions of such leaders with the members of their groups start with the provision of a collective good and end with slavery. But this line of argument

[17] These factors cannot be treated formally in terms of our present model of "closed" social structures. They are mentioned here only as possible areas for further analysis.

[18] Although the leader may exploitatively extract resources from the members in order to maximize his surplus, this says nothing about the uses to which he may put this surplus. So, for example, he may provide himself with extravagant palaces or, if he has a high b, provide the society with extravagant levels of collective goods.

is not meant to show any necessary relationship between political entrepreneurship and slavery. Such factors as the size of the b term, revenue from donations, the marginal costs of collecting additional taxes, and the leader's own utility valuations of certain collective goods will operate to overcome this *tendency* toward exploitation.

Moreover, this discussion applies only to situations in which there is no competition for the leadership role. In this sense, the leader is all-powerful, and our conclusions may be thought of as a reformulation of Lord Action's famous remark: "Power tends to corrupt; absolute power corrupts absolutely." Competition for the occupancy of the leadership role, however, may open up alternatives for the membership and improve their position. But competition also introduces major new problems of analysis and complicates the theoretical analysis. The next chapter, therefore, will deal with the manner in which competition affects the relations between a political leader and the members of his group.

CHAPTER THREE

Competitive Politics

COMPETITION AND OPPOSITION

The fact that the role occupied by the political leaders is profitable will often be sufficient to motivate other members of the social structure to seek to obtain profits from the supply of collective goods.

Economic and Political Competition

Micro-economic theory recognizes explicitly two types of competition among entrepreneurs who supply private goods to tap a pool of potential profits. First, an economic entrepreneur can compete by producing the same product that others produce with the objective of capturing a share of the market for the product in question. Second, such entrepreneurs may compete by differentiating their products from those of their competitors, thereby establishing themselves in new markets. Competition among political leaders who supply collective goods, however, will characteristically take different forms than competition among economic entrepreneurs. While political leaders may compete through diversification or "product differentiation," they are quite unlikely to vie for shares of a given market.

Competition among suppliers of a given private good is predicated upon the fact that such goods can be supplied to individual consumers on an exclusionary basis.

That is, the consumption of a private good by one individual does not satisfy the demand of other individuals for that good. As a result, a competitor may often be able to gain a profit in a given private-good market by supplying a certain number of units of the good over and above those supplied by the original producer. Traditional economic analyses of the supply of private goods are based on the assumption that given some specified level of aggregate demand, cost functions will determine the size of any particular producer in a market. When the original producer experiences decreasing returns with increasing size before the demand for the good is fully met, there will be a potential for successful competition. In more technical terms, the notion of increasing marginal cost is employed in economic analyses to explain the occurrence of competition among producers of an undifferentiated product. This is generally assumed to occur at some point, thereby preventing pure economic monopolies from being viable under most circumstances.

Considerations of this kind, however, are much less likely to play a role in competition among producers of collective goods. To demonstrate this, we will assume (1) that at least some of the collective goods in question are characterized by jointness of supply (i.e. all members of the group share the same unit of the good), and (2) that the consumption of the good by one member does not decrease the utility other members receive from consuming the good (i.e. there are no crowding effects).[1]

---

[1] For discussions of the conceptual issues associated with these assumptions, see John G. Head, "Public Goods and Public Policy," *Public Finance* 17 (1962), 197–219, and John G. Head and Carl S. Shoup, "Public Goods, Private Goods, and Ambiguous Goods," *The Economic Journal* 79 (1969), 567–572. The

Given these conditions, it is possible to clarify the differences between economic competition and political competition with a simple example.

Consider a situation in which there are three individuals, each of whom values a particular private good, Y. The first individual, i, is willing to buy one unit of Y for \$3, another unit for \$2, a third unit for \$1, and is uninterested in a fourth unit regardless of the price. Assume for the sake of simplicity that the other individuals, j and k, are similarly disposed. Then, the behavior of each of the individuals with respect to the consumption of Y can be summarized by the demand curve shown in Figure I. And the market for Y, as assessed by an economic entrepreneur, is the horizontal sum of the demand curves of the three individuals shown in Figure II. Thus, in the example, an entrepreneur can expect to sell different units of Y to i, j, and k. He can, therefore, sell three units of Y if the price is \$3, six units if the price is \$2, and nine units if the price is \$1. And no more than nine units can be sold. If a particular producer of Y can supply only four units of the good at a price of \$2, there may be room for another producer to enter the market and supply two additional units at \$2 or an even greater number of units at a lower price. The potential for a second firm to enter the market arises because the overall quantity of the good demanded depends on the number of consumers rather than the behavior of any individual consumer. As the number of

---

introduction of these assumptions means that our analysis of political competition deals with a set of limited cases. Norman Frohlich and Joe A. Oppenheimer are now exploring various possibilities for relaxing these assumptions and extending the analysis of political competition formulated in this book to additional cases.

consumers increases, the aggregate quantity of the good demanded also increases. And the greater the aggregate quantity of the good demanded, the larger must be the scale of any producer that satisfies these demands fully and, therefore, the more likely it is that a single producer will reach the point of decreasing returns to scale. If

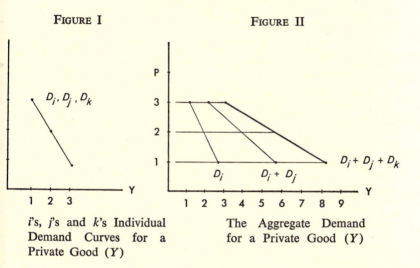

FIGURE I

FIGURE II

i's, j's and k's Individual Demand Curves for a Private Good (Y)

The Aggregate Demand for a Private Good (Y)

this point is reached before the demand is fully satisfied, a competitor will be able to make a profit by entering the market. All other things being equal, then, the greater the number of consumers of a given private good, the more chance there will be for an additional producer to make a profit by competing for a share of the market.

But what happens if the entrepreneur is a political leader who supplies an indivisible collective good which is not affected by crowding? Assume that each of the three individuals values the collective good, X, identically to Y. Then, although each individual's demand curve for X looks exactly like the demand curve shown in Figure I, the aggregate demand curve that the leader faces is entirely different. In the case of private goods, the aggregate demand curve was the horizontal sum of the individual demand curves; for indivisible collective goods, it is the vertical sum.[2] Supplying the good, X, means that all three individuals will receive it automatically and that contributions made by any of the individuals will go for the *same* good. Thus, assuming no crowding effects, with an increase in the number of individuals the overall quantity of the good demanded does not increase as rapidly as in the first case when the number of individuals who demand the good increases. But the potential price the group of individuals is willing to pay for each unit of the good (ignoring strategic interactions for the moment) increases more rapidly. Under the circumstances, the first unit of X can be "sold" for $9, the second for $6, the third for $3 (see Figure III). In economic terms, a vertical aggregation of "downward sloping" demand curves will always be less elastic than a horizontal aggregation of the same curves.[3]

Under these conditions, the potential competitor to a political leader is faced with a different prospect than the economic competitor. Most important, the rate of

[2] Paul A. Samuelson, "Diagrammatic Exposition of a Theory of Public Expenditures," *Review of Economics and Statistics* 37 (Nov. 1955), 350–356.

[3] This argument concerning the differences between economic and political competition hinges on the distinction between horizontal and vertical summation in the construction of aggregate demand curves. When a number of downward sloping demand curves are summed horizontally, the aggregate curve will always have a slope that is less than that of the flattest individual curve included in the aggregate. That is, the summing of individual demand curves makes the aggregate curve flatter and flatter. Vertical summation, on the other hand, has the opposite effect. The result of a vertical summation will be a curve with a slope greater than that of the steepest individual curve in the aggregate (cf. Figs. II and III).

change of the quantity of the collective good demanded as a function of the number of members in the group will be small. Then, there will be no *a priori* reason to assume that the original producer will reach a point

FIGURE III

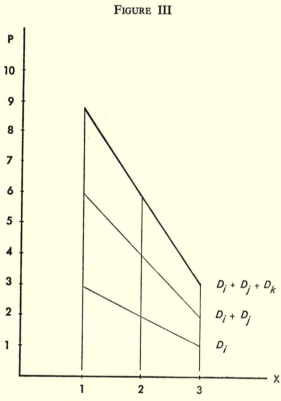

The Aggregate Demand for a Collective Good (X)

of decreasing returns before fully satisfying the group's demands for the good in question. As a result, the supply of collective goods which exhibit no crowding effects will generate natural monopolies, and there is apt to be no room for a second entrepreneur who attempts to compete for a share of the "market" associated with the good in question.

The implications of this distinction are not difficult to spell out. Competition between suppliers of collective goods which do not exhibit crowding effects will be fundamentally different from competition arising from the supply of private goods.[4] The former will tend to involve the development of monopolies, while the latter will generally lead to the sharing of markets among competitors. In addition, the greatest profit in the supply of any given collective good will usually stem from supplying the first units of the good. The overall quantity of the good supplied will not change much even with relatively large fluctuations in costs. The surplus that the supplier can obtain, therefore, becomes primarily a function of the number of people who consume the good.

Opposition

The profits reaped by a political leader will often cause other individuals to aspire to become leaders themselves. In seeking to make a profit from the supply of collective goods, such individuals will have to consider two distinct options.[5] First, a competitor can promise to supply a collective good that no member of the social structure regards as a substitute for the good supplied

[4] It may well be, however, that some of the more "sordid" aspects of the activities of economic entrepreneurs can be analyzed in terms of competition for leadership roles. This follows from the analysis of the relationship between the roles in Chapter Two, pp. 57–58.

[5] The assumption that aspiring leaders do not engage in unprofitable activities is a strong one. It insures that individuals do not compete for the leadership role by spending their own private resources in the hope of eventually replacing the leader.

by the incumbent leader. Second, he can promise to supply a good that is regarded by everyone as a substitute for the good already supplied by the incumbent.[6]

The first case raises no serious complications. Here the situation facing the aspiring leader is analytically the same as that which the original leader faced before any collective goods were supplied in the social structure.[7] It was argued in Chapter One that any individual who estimates that he can collect sufficient resources to enjoy a surplus may set up a collection organization, supply the collective good, and keep the surplus. This basic argument continues to hold even when there is already a successful political leader in the social structure. Thus, if some individual can make a profit by supplying a collective good that is not a substitute for a good already being supplied, he may establish himself as a second political leader on the basis of the new collective good.

The second case, however, raises a variety of questions. Any individual who seeks to make a profit by promising to supply a collective good that is generally regarded as a substitute for the good already provided

---

[6] These two cases are polar opposites. Intermediate cases may also occur in which the collective good promised by the competitor is regarded as a substitute for that supplied by the incumbent leader by some but not all of the members of the social structure. Intermediate cases of this kind would raise substantial analytic complexities that would carry us too far afield for the purposes of this book. It would be interesting, however, to consider cases of this kind in future work based on the theory set forth in this book.

[7] If the demands for the good supplied by the incumbent and the aspiring leader are independent of each other, the supply of one will affect the supply of the other only through income effects and the types of efficiency questions discussed in Chapter Two.

by the incumbent leader is faced with a different situation. We will call such a leader an *opposition leader*. The opponent's promise to supply a substitute collective good in the future produces an alternative or a choice for the ordinary member of the social structure. Such a choice is, in itself, a collective good. If the alternative is supplied to one member of the social structure, it will automatically be supplied to all members. Thus, the collective good supplied by an opposition leader, so long as he remains in opposition, is a promised alternative to the program of the incumbent leader. It will, therefore, be profitable for an individual to become an opposition leader whenever he can collect more for the supply of a future alternative than he expends in providing this alternative on a credible basis.[8]

It must be noted that the profitability of supplying opposition will be affected by strategic interaction between the competitors and the members of the social

---

[8] Relaxing the condition discussed in note 5, it is possible to imagine situations in which some individual supplies collective goods to the members of a social structure out of his own private resources in the hope of undermining the political leader by making him redundant and eventually occupying his vacated role, thereby recouping his investment and making a profit in the following time periods. Behavior of this kind would be the political equivalent of the efforts of large firms to destroy their competition by selling at a loss for a period of time in order to enjoy a monopoly in subsequent periods.

The original resources put into political activities by an individual of this kind would be a form of investment. As a result, the individual could be expected to calculate the expected returns to his investment over several time periods and to compare these returns with those he could get from other uses of his resources. Whether or not he would choose to enter the political arena in any given situation would be determined by the outcome of these comparisons.

structure.[9] For this reason, the potential for profit in the supply of opposition can never be ascertained with certainty. One factor that will have a substantial impact on the success of any effort to make a profit from the supply of opposition, however, will be the sources of revenue relied upon by the competitors. That is, different combinations of sources of revenue will generate different patterns of strategic behavior affecting the profitability of opposition. As a result, some combinations of sources of revenue will offer the opposition leader a considerably better chance of collecting enough resources to make a profit than others. By way of illustration, consider the following two cases.

First, both the political leader and the opponent may levy taxes simultaneously on the same people.[10] Since it is only possible to extract taxes from individuals through the threat or use of sanctions, competitors who rely on taxes from the same individuals will often experience strong incentives to cut into each other's tax base in their efforts to maintain profitable operations. For example, if one leader can extract $1 in taxes from a given individual while a second leader can extract $2

[9] A more systematic analysis of the inevitable occurrence of strategic interaction in such situations can be found in Chapter Five.

[10] As before, both taxes and extortions are subsumed under the general heading of taxation in outlining the principal arguments of this chapter. Note, however, that extortions raise problems of strategic behavior, whereas taxes as defined here do not (although one could imagine alternative definitions of taxation which would introduce the potential for strategic interaction). This is so because extortions involve collective goods, whereas taxes are based on private-good exchanges. Wherever extortions are relevant, therefore, it should be remembered that the exact amount of resources collected through this process will be a function of strategic interactions.

75

from the same individual, the second leader will have a possibility of gaining up to $1 in voluntary contributions plus $2 in taxes if he can guarantee to protect the individual from the first leader. It may often be possible to supply protection of this kind on a profitable basis. That is, it may well cost a leader less to supply protection than the value of the additional revenue such activities can bring him.[11] This is true because the coercive organization that the leader creates to extract taxes is likely to be similar to the type of organization required to oppose another leader's taxing organization.[12] This suggests that there will often be a tendency toward monopoly in the collection of taxes, at least within certain spheres of influence. It does not mean, however, that opponents will not be able to obtain more restricted forms of tax revenue (e.g. from some subset of the social structure that the leader cannot protect efficiently).

Strategic interaction between the competitors in a situation of this kind is almost assured, but it can take a variety of forms. One clear-cut possibility is a fight to the finish in which one of the competitors is ultimately excluded from the political arena. By the same token, however, the incumbent leader and the opponent may well discover great mutual advantages in various forms of collusion designed to maximize their combined profits as well as to preserve the political arena itself from destruction. Collusion of this type may take many forms,

[11] This is true whether protection is supplied as a collective good or as a private good.

[12] The profitability of such efforts to acquire exclusive taxing rights can be analyzed in terms of the "viability" models developed by Kenneth Boulding in his *Conflict and Defense* (New York 1962), Chapter 4. In order to make use of these models in the context of the present analysis, however, it would be necessary to extend them to take into account individualistic utility valuations.

ranging from various types of profit-sharing agreements to arrangements aimed at fixing the mode of competition that will be employed.[13]

Second, both the incumbent leader and the opponent may rely primarily on donations. Such situations raise great uncertainties concerning the profitability of supplying opposition. To begin with, the emergence of an opposition leader produces a dilemma for the ordinary members of the social structure. As far as the individual member is concerned, either the incumbent or the opponent can satisfy his demand for collective goods in the next time period. However, each member must make a decision about which leader will receive his donation, and take into account the probable behavior of the other members of the social structure as well as the promises of the opposition leader. This is true because the behavior of others will have a substantial impact on the actual supply of collective goods and, therefore, on the expected-value calculations of the individual member. Under these conditions, strategic behavior will occur among the ordinary members regarding both the size and the distribution of their donations. Moreover, in their efforts to obtain the larger share of the donations, the competitors will engage in strategic interactions with each other and with the ordinary members on the basis of appeals, pledges, and promises for the future. As a result, there will be a real possibility that the members' donations will split between the incumbent and the opponent in such a way that no collective goods at all will be supplied.

In addition, if the substitute offered by the opponent

[13] A mode of competition is the combination of tactics employed by all the competitors in a competitive situation. A fuller discussion of the problems associated with modes of competition can be found on pp. 98–99.

involves a promise of greater efficiency than that characteristic of the operations of the incumbent leader, the rational member must consider the level at which he should continue his donations. "If the goods can be supplied more efficiently," he may reason, "can they not get along with a smaller donation on my part, or even without any donation from me at all?" As a result, any promise on the part of an opponent involving increased efficiency will change the information available to the ordinary member and may well lead to a substantial reduction in his donations, and this will affect the profitability of both the incumbent leader and the opponent.

An opposition leader takes great risks, therefore, when he promises to supply a substitute for the collective goods provided by the incumbent leader in cases where both rely primarily on donations. In the long run, one or the other of the competitors may win, thereby driving the loser out of the competition. Alternatively, the effects of strategic interactions may make it impossible for either the incumbent or the opponent to make a profit in a situation of this kind.

The potential profitability of opposition in this second case, however, may be improved by the introduction of some mechanism that increases the probability that some collective goods will be supplied no matter how the donations split between the competitors. Any mechanism that differentiates the resources needed to compete for the occupancy of the role of political leader from those required to supply the collective goods would have this effect.

Define a decision rule as any agreed-upon mechanism that specifies the minimum conditions in terms of which competition for the leadership position is decided. Then any decision rule will specify a numeraire resource or a set of numeraire resources in terms of which victory is determined. A decision rule will also establish the transformation functions governing the translation of various other resources into numeraire resources. Thus, a specific decision rule will define the minimum set of all resources which will guarantee victory in a competitive situation (i.e. the minimum winning coalition). Decision rules in democracies, for example, define votes as the numeraire resource and often stipulate a simple majority as the minimum winning coalition. In any given democracy, a minimum winning coalition requires the control of other resources only insofar as they are necessary to obtain votes.

An opposition leader who relies on donations may make a profit by supplying opposition when the numeraire resources and those other resources required to obtain numeraire resources are different from those needed to supply the collective goods provided by the incumbent leader. This is so because the ordinary members of the social structure could donate substantial quantities of these resources to the opposition leader without endangering the supply of collective goods already provided by the incumbent leader. That is, contributions for the collective good of opposition would not compete with contributions for other collective goods valued by the members of the social structure.[14]

[14] Even though a specific decision rule exists in a social structure, various members may attempt to change it or operate outside the arrangements it sets forth. Thus, in democracies based on universal suffrage, some may attempt to gain office through insurrection. And in hereditary monarchies, some may try to acquire the position of king through assassination. Actions of this kind on the part of individuals will be taken on the basis of cost-benefit calculations. Here the analysis has been restricted to situations in which the members find it expedient to abide by an established decision rule. Deviations from existing rules and calculations concerning efforts to change decision rules are discussed on pp. 98–99.

Opposition as a Career

Since the role of opponent may be a profitable one, it is important to consider the role premise of the opposition leader. This role premise will include a variety of terms that are similar to those found in the role premise of the political leader.

Outcomes for the Opponent

Any opposition leader, B, will assess his prospects in terms of three possible outcomes.[15] First, he may remain in opposition, obtaining whatever surplus accrues to the role of opponent. Second, he may take over the position of the political leader, thereby capturing the leader's surplus. Third, he may withdraw from political competition altogether and suffer any consequences this withdrawal may entail. Each of these outcomes will have a probability associated with it in any given situation. We can designate B's estimation of the probabilities of each of these alternatives as follows: he may remain in opposition with probability $P_B(L'_B)$, become the political leader with probability $P_B(L_B)$, or withdraw from political competition altogether with probability $P_B(E_B)$.[16] The utility function of the opposition leader with respect to his future prospects will therefore take the form of an expected-value calculation. His expected utility for the future will be the sum of the utility he would derive from his three possible outcomes times the

[15] A logical implication of this analysis is the possibility of competition for the role of opposition leader, and so forth. In order to avoid this development, we will assume in the present discussion that there is no competition for the role of opposition leader. This assumption can be relaxed, however, in cases where it is found to be unrealistic.

[16] Note that we assume that these three outcomes are mutually exclusive and exhaustive. Hence, $P_B(L') + P_B(L) + P_B(E) = 1$.

probability of each. This can be expressed algebraically as:

$$U_B = U_B(L'_B)P_B(L'_B) + U_B(L_B)P_B(L_B) \\ + U_B(E_B)P_B(E_B) \qquad (3.1)$$

where $U_B(L'_B)$ is the utility he derives from the role of opponent, $U_B(L_B)$ the utility of being the leader, and $U_B(E_B)$ the utility of being excluded from the political arena altogether. Rational action on the part of an opposition leader with respect to the future, then, would consist in maximizing the value of this expression.

But this expression is based on an excessively restrictive representation of the opponent's future alternatives. The opposition leader need not estimate his probability of remaining in opposition once and for all, weigh this against the probability of becoming leader for all future time periods, and so forth. Rather, he will estimate the probabilities associated with the various outcomes in the next time period and calculate the utilities he can expect from each of these positions. He will also consider the outcomes that he faces in the time period which follows the next time period, and so forth. In this fashion, the opposition leader will weigh the various outcomes on the basis of their respective probabilities and utility pay-offs for each of the time periods in the future. With this factor in mind, we can restate the general form of the opposition leader's role premise as one that includes time-period analysis. The expected utility of the opposition leader therefore becomes the summation of his expected incomes for each of the relevant time periods. This can be expressed algebraically as:

$$U_B = \sum_{t=1}^{m} \Big(U_B(L'_B)P_B(L'_B) + U_B(L_B)P_B(L_B) \\ + U_B(E_B)P_B(E_B) \Big)_t \qquad (3.2)$$

Rational behavior on the part of the opposition leader will consist in maximizing this expression. That is, he attempts to get the most profit he can over the time he expects to be politically active.

The fact that the opponent operates in this fashion forces the leader to do likewise. With the introduction of competition, the leader's tenure in office becomes uncertain, and he must contemplate a future that includes the possibility of losing office. Under conditions of competition, then, the role premise of the leader must be altered to take this possibility into account. Thus, the expected-value income of the political leader becomes the summation of the expected income from continuing in the leadership role, the expected income from becoming an opposition leader, and the expected income from being excluded from the political arena altogether. And all these possible outcomes must be considered over time. As in the case of the rational opposition leader, therefore, rational behavior on the part of a political leader A will consist in maximizing the sum of these income streams over time. This can be expressed algebraically as:[17]

$$U_A = \sum_{t=1}^{m} \Big(U_A(L_A)P_A(L_A) + U_A(L'_A)P_A(L'_A) + U_A(E_A)P_A(E_A) \Big)_t \qquad (3.3)$$

In attempting to maximize this expression, the political leader will be faced with the possibility of making a variety of trade-offs. In general, however, he will have to calculate the advantages of trading off probabilities in the present or future for utility payoffs in the present or future. Under the circumstances, his behavior will

[17] Note that this expression is almost identical in form to the expression for the opposition leader's role premise.

be determined in large measure by strategic interactions among himself, the opposition, and the ordinary members.

Implications for the "Downsian Politician"

One conclusion that flows from the preceding analysis is that Anthony Downs's well-known model of the politician is a special case of our political leader.[18] Downs hypothesized that the politician will always attempt to maximize his probability of acquiring or staying in office. Such a conception assumes that the politician has no ability to manipulate his surplus in any given time period and, therefore, is unable to trade off increases in his surplus for decreases in his probabilities of staying in office or acquiring office.[19] It also precludes the possibility of a politician's trading off probabilities of winning in one time period for probabilities of winning in other time periods.

In addition, many of the important strategic concerns of the political leader, as we have conceptualized his role, will be related to the size of the surplus he enjoys and to his ability to manipulate this surplus. A variety of consequences for the social structure will follow from the manner in which the political leader behaves to maximize his surplus. However Downs's idea that politicians act only to maximize their probability of holding office precludes the analysis of these consequences.

[18] Anthony Downs, *An Economic Theory of Democracy* (New York 1957).

[19] Our analysis implies that politicians will be willing to trade increased payoffs in one time period for a greater probability of losing office in a subsequent time period if such trade-offs maximize their expected surplus. It follows that politicians will sometimes consciously shorten their tenure in office in return for immediate gains.

83

THE VALUE OF BEING IN OPPOSITION

Earlier it was asserted that the opposition leader expects to derive some utility from occupying the role of opponent. (This source of utility was represented as $U_B(L'_B)$ in equation 3.1.) A comparison of this source of utility for the occupant of an opposition role with the utility an individual receives from occupying a leadership role brings to light the parallel structures of the two roles.

The opposition leader's sources of revenues and costs are analytically similar to those of the political leader. Just as the political leader may expect voluntary contributions from the ordinary members in return for the supply of collective goods, the opposition leader may expect contributions for similar activities. Opposition itself is a collective good supplied by anyone who opposes an incumbent leader.[20] Moreover, the opposition leader who promises to supply additional collective goods may be able to obtain donations from ordinary members who hope that he will be able to implement his promises to their ultimate benefit. Therefore, one of the terms in the opposition leader's utility valuation will be the amount of donations he can obtain.[21]

Voluntary contributions to the opposition leader will be just as uncertain as those to the political leader since they will be heavily influenced by strategic interactions

[20] Among other things, this means that opposition will always be nonoptimally supplied. This conclusion follows directly from the argument set forth on pp. 59–62.

[21] Note, however, that the argument on pp. 77–78 indicates that an opposition leader is likely to face great difficulties in collecting substantial donations by promising to supply collective goods more efficiently when the incumbent leader relies primarily on donations as a source of revenue.

among all of the actors in the social structure. A more reliable source of potential revenue for the opposition leader will be taxation based on his ability to impose sanctions on the members of the social structure or some subset of these members. Taxation will provide a significant source of revenue for the opposition to the extent that the opposition leader can construct a coercive organization capable of operating despite the existence of a comparable organization controlled by the political leader.[22]

Another potential source of revenue for the opposition leader is profits from the sale of positively valued private goods to some or all of the members of the social structure. As noted in the discussion of the political leader's role premise, actions along these lines can be assessed in terms of standard economic analysis. Consequently, we will omit any detailed analysis of this term here.

There will also be several types of cost associated with the opposition leader's role. He will have to supply some collection organization to gather revenues, whether it is a coercive or a noncoercive agency. In most cases, he will also have to bear the costs of providing the opposition, which he has promised, in some credible form. And he may consider it necessary, in order to maintain his position, to supply some collective goods other than opposition itself to the membership of the social structure or some subset of the membership. All of these factors will be costs in his estimation of the utility of opposition, although he may recoup some of his expenses through the receipt of contributions for contracts relating to provision of the goods he supplies. Such contributions would

[22] Under most conditions, the scope of the opposition leader's coercive organization will be more restricted than that of the political leader. Thus, for example, the opponent may be able to tax some subset of the members of the social structure.

85

be analogous to the added revenue the leader may receive. Finally, like the political leader, the opponent may receive some utility simply from presiding over his administrative apparatus.

In summary, then, the basic terms that the opposition leader will have to consider in evaluating the utility he can derive from opposition in one time period will be: the utility he himself derives from the collective goods he supplies, $U_B(X_B)$, donations, $\sum_{j=1}^{n} D_j(B)$, and taxation, $\sum_{j=1}^{n} T_j(B)$, on the revenue side, and the costs of a collection organization, $C(O_B)$, as well as the costs of supplying collective goods, $C(X_B)$, on the cost side. These costs may be modified by the utility he gets from administration $b_B[C(O_B) + C(X_B)]$. Thus, the utility the opposition leader can expect from the occupancy of the opponent's role in any given time period can be expressed algebraically as:

$$U_B(L'_B) = U_B(X_B) + \sum_{j=1}^{n} D_j(B) + \sum_{j=1}^{n} T_j(B)$$
$$- (1 - b_B)[C(O_B) + C(X_B)] \qquad (3.4)$$

This equation takes into account only those factors that result directly from the opponent's activities as opposition leader. Given the assumptions set forth in Chapter One, however, the opposition leader is also a member of the social structure, and he therefore experiences the benefits and costs that membership entails even while acting as opponent. As a member, he receives utility from any collective goods the political leader supplies, and he may receive profitable contracts from the leader. At the same time, the opposition leader may be subjected to taxation by the political leader, and he may even find it worthwhile to donate some resources to the leader. As a result, these terms will also figure in the opposition leader's estimation of the utility he can derive from occupying the role of opponent. These considerations can be formally included in equation 3.4 by adding the term $U_B(L_A)$.[23] The result is the net utility the opposition leader can expect from the occupancy of the role of opponent during one time period. This can be expressed algebraically as:

$$U_B(L'_B) = U_B(X_B) + \sum_{j=1}^{n} D_j(B) + \sum_{j=1}^{n} T_j(B)$$
$$- (1 - b_B)[C(O_B) + C(X_B)] + U_B(L_A) \qquad (3.5)$$

Whenever this expression is greater than zero, the activities associated with opposition itself will be profitable.[24]

The rational opposition leader will always act to maximize the value of equation 3.2, which contains equation 3.5. That is, the strategy of the opposition leader will be to maximize his income whether he wants it for purposes of acquiring the leadership position, for its own sake, or for other ends. In all cases, however, the opposition leader will draw contributions from the members

[23] The components of this term are directly analogous to the factors in equation 1.11, which defines the utility the individual member derives from the leader of the social structure.

[24] This conclusion goes directly against that reached by R. Curry and L. Wade, *A Theory of Political Exchange* (Englewood Cliffs, N.J. 1968), 48. They argue that "until and unless he is successful in achieving office, the competing politician suffers a net loss of welfare." In addition, Downs's analysis of the politician as an individual who tries to maximize his probability of gaining office is consistent with the argument of Curry and Wade. Our analysis of the potential profits associated with the role of opposition leader contradicts these formulations.

of the social structure.[25] In the next section, therefore, changes brought about in the role premise of the ordinary member by the emergence of an opposition leader will be examined.

THE BEHAVIOR OF MEMBERS IN COMPETITIVE SITUATIONS

Consider the effects of opposition on the decision of the individual member concerning his donations. To do so, assume for the purposes of discussion that there is only one opposition leader.[26]

The Member's Valuation of Opposition

Any individual member, concerned with the utility he can expect to derive from the leader of the social structure, must take into account the possibility that either of the competitors, A and B, may be the political leader in the next time period.[27] Specifically, his expected

---

[25] This follows from the original assumption (p. 30) regarding the isolation of social structures.

[26] The analysis would have to be modified considerably to take account of the existence of more than one opponent. Specifically, we would have to consider the whole problem of coalition formation. There are several reasons to focus here on the special two-person case, however, even though the possibility of forming coalitions would modify the behavior of the ordinary member as well as that of the leader and opposition leaders. First, the principal variables affecting the response of members to competition can be outlined and assessed more readily in the two-person case. Second, many of the critical variables affecting competition in two-person situations will be important in n-person situations as well.

[27] Here it is assumed that the members of the social structure consider only the short-run future in making their decisions. That is, they make donations today essentially to affect the benefits they will receive tomorrow. To take into account long-

value from political leadership will be the sum of the utility he would get from each competitor were that competitor victorious[28] times his estimation of the probability that each competitor will be victorious:

$$U_j(L) = U_j(L_{A+B}) = U_j(L_A)P_j(L_A) + U_j(L_B)P_j(L_B) \tag{3.6}$$

But the individual member confronted with the existence of two competitors for the leadership role will have to take into account factors other than the utility he could derive from each competitor were he to become the political leader; each competitor is also a potential opposition leader. The contribution that the opposition leader can make to the member's utility function can be described in a fashion similar to the contribution of the political leader:

$$U_j(L') = U_j(L'_{A+B}) = U_j(L'_A)P_j(L'_A) \\ + U_j(L'_B)P_j(L'_B) \tag{3.7}$$

Similarly, the individual member must consider the utility that would accrue to him were either of the competitors excluded from the political arena altogether:

$$U_j(E) = U_j(E_{A+B}) = U_j(E_A)P_j(E_A) \\ + U_j(E_B)P_j(E_B) \tag{3.8}$$

All of these considerations can be incorporated into a single equation that defines the utility that the individual

---

run calculations, a more complicated time-period analysis can be constructed by employing the notion of a discount rate. This would permit an analysis of the relationship between donations today and long-run payoffs as a problem of investments, which must earn more than the interest on savings to be considered profitable. Although an analysis of this type raises no analytic difficulties, it would detract from the main thrust of our present argument.

[28] $U_i(L)$ is defined in Chapter One in equation 1.8.

member can expect to derive from the entire political process.

$$U_j = U_j(L) + U_j(L') + U_j(E) \qquad (3.9)$$

The removal of either competitor from the political arena, however, would result from the actions of one or the other of the competitors. That is, the exclusion of one of the competitors can be viewed as a collective good supplied to the members of the social structure, and the utility the individual member might derive from this action would be a function of the program of one of the competitors. Note, however, that this collective good may be supplied by either the political leader or the opposition leader. As a result, the utility the individual member derives from the exclusion of one of the competitors may be subsumed under either the $U_j(L)$ term or the $U_j(L')$ term in equation 3.9. With this in mind, we can reformulate the general utility function of the individual member as:

$$U_j = U_j(L) + U_j(L') \qquad (3.10)$$

or in expanded form, substituting equations 3.6 and 3.7 into equation 3.10, as:

$$U_j = U_j(L_A)P_j(L_A) + U_j(L_B)P_j(L_B) \\ + U_j(L'_A)P_j(L'_A) + U_j(L'_B)P_j(L'_B) \qquad (3.11)$$

This is the expected utility the member obtains as a result of A's and B's competition for occupancy of the leadership role.

Contributing to Competitors

With the introduction of competition, the individual member, who could previously hope only to influence the program of a single leader through his donations, acquires the ability to influence the programs of two competitors. And he is also able to affect each competitor's probability of acquiring or retaining the positions of political leader and opposition leader. Under these conditions, the individual member must consider how to allocate his donations among the competitors as well as what amounts to donate. If we continue to assume that there are only two competitors, the member's total donations can be divided into his donations to A, $D_j(A)$, and his donations to B, $D_j(B)$.[29]

The individual member will continue to donate to A or B until the value of the additional benefits he can hope to secure through an additional donation is fully offset by what he gives up in making the donations. That is, when additional donations to A or B no longer pay for themselves in terms of the benefits they produce, the member will stop donating. Algebraically, this point can be represented as:[30]

$$\frac{\partial U_j}{\partial D_j(A)} = 0 \qquad (3.12)$$

$$\frac{\partial U_j}{\partial D_j(B)} = 0 \qquad (3.13)$$

[29] For the sake of simplicity, assume here that a_j's decision regarding his donations to A does not directly affect his decision about his donations to B. The only link between the two decisions, then, is the effect of each on the utility a_j expects to receive from the leadership of the social structure.

[30] In these equations, $\dfrac{\partial U_j}{\partial D_j(A)}$ means a change in a_j's utility brought about by an additional donation to A, while $\dfrac{\partial U_j}{\partial D_j(B)}$ means a change in a_j's utility resulting from an additional donation to B. In both cases, the change indicated is that which occurs when all other independent variables are held constant. At maxima, these rates of change (or partial derivatives) are zero and returns from contributions are declining. The rules governing the derivatives of products and sums are applicable to partial derivatives. These are described in note 26 of Chapter One.

But remember that the general utility function of the individual member (equation 3.11) is:

$$U_j = U_j(L_A)P_j(L_A) + U_j(L_B)P_j(L_B)$$
$$+ U_j(L'_A)P_j(L'_A) + U_j(L'_B)P_j(L'_B)$$

As a result, the utility a_j derives from a donation to A (or B) will be determined by the way the donation affects all of the terms in his general utility function. Consider first the impact of a donation on the utility a_j derives from the leadership role. On the one hand, a donation to A might affect the program A would offer as the political leader and, therefore, the utility the member hopes to receive if A is victorious. The expected value of such a change can be expressed algebraically as $\dfrac{\partial U_j(L_A)}{\partial D_j(A)}P_j(L_A)$. On the other hand, a_j's donation may affect the probability that A will in fact be victorious and therefore be in a position to carry out the programs expected of him. The value of this effect of a donation can be expressed as $\dfrac{\partial P_j(L_A)}{\partial D_j(A)}U_j(L_A)$. A donation to A that affects the probability that A will be victorious, however, also affects the probability that B will be victorious and, therefore, the expected value of B's leadership programs to the donor. This can be expressed as $\dfrac{\partial P_j(L_B)}{\partial D_j(A)}U_j(L_B)$. And any such modification a_j causes in B's fortunes may well produce a response from B in the form of a change in his (B's) leadership programs. The expected value of this effect can be written as $\dfrac{\partial U_j(L_B)}{\partial D_j(A)}P_j(L_B)$. By the same token, a donation on the part of an individual member can induce four types of change in the utility he receives from the occupant of the role of opposition leader. Since these terms are directly analogous to those described above in the case of the political leader, there is no need to spell them out here.

92

In summary, then, a donation to A will have eight effects on the utility of the individual donor:

$$\frac{\partial U_j}{\partial D_j(A)} = \frac{\partial U_j(L_A)}{\partial D_j(A)} P_j(L_A) + \frac{\partial P_j(L_A)}{\partial D_j(A)} U_j(L_A)$$
$$+ \frac{\partial U_j(L_B)}{\partial D_j(A)} P_j(L_B) + \frac{\partial P_j(L_B)}{\partial D_j(A)} U_j(L_B)$$
$$+ \frac{\partial U_j(L'_A)}{\partial D_j(A)} P_j(L'_A) + \frac{\partial P_j(L'_A)}{\partial D_j(A)} U_j(L'_A)$$
$$+ \frac{\partial U_j(L'_B)}{\partial D_j(A)} P_j(L'_B) + \frac{\partial P_j(L'_B)}{\partial D_j(A)} U_j(L'_B) \qquad (3.14)$$

And a donation to B will also have eight effects on the utility of the individual donor:

$$\frac{\partial U_j}{\partial D_j(B)} = \frac{\partial U_j(L_A)}{\partial D_j(B)} P_j(L_A) + \frac{\partial P_j(L_A)}{\partial D_j(B)} U_j(L_A)$$
$$+ \frac{\partial U_j(L_B)}{\partial D_j(B)} P_j(L_B) + \frac{\partial P_j(L_B)}{\partial D_j(B)} U_j(L_B)$$
$$+ \frac{\partial U_j(L'_A)}{\partial D_j(B)} P_j(L'_A) + \frac{\partial P_j(L'_A)}{\partial D_j(B)} U_j(L'_A)$$
$$+ \frac{\partial U_j(L'_B)}{\partial D_j(B)} P_j(L'_B) + \frac{\partial P_j(L'_B)}{\partial D_j(B)} U_j(L'_B) \qquad (3.15)$$

Under these conditions, individual members will find themselves in equilibrium with respect to their donations when equations 3.14 and 3.15 are equal to zero and, therefore, to each other (as specified in equations 3.12 and 3.13). When these conditions are met, the costs associated with further donations to any of the competitors will completely and exactly offset the benefits to be gained from such donations. The individual member who meets these conditions with respect to the allocation of his donations between the competitors will also be in equilibrium with respect to the overall size of his donations. In other words, the member will be in equilibrium with respect to the overall size of his donations when

$dU_j/dD_j = 0$, and this condition will be met whenever the other conditions stipulated above are met.[31]

Equilibrium in this sense is likely to occur only when the individual donates to both competitors (though rarely in equal amounts). In fact, the special case of donations to only one of the contestants will occur only when the marginal cost of donating to one of them always outweighs the benefits that accrue to the donor. This could occur when the donor views the program of one contestant as extremely unappealing and inflexible in contrast to the program of the other contestant. Such a specialization of donations could also occur if one of the competitors is thought to be a hopeless loser and is not valued highly by the donor as an opposition leader. Finally, the individual may be unaware of the potentialities in giving to both contestants with the result that he donates only to increase the probability of victory of his preferred candidate. In general, the larger the size of a member's donations, the more likely he is to have access to relevent information regarding the possible benefits of donations. This may explain why the larger and more regular donors in the United States are more likely to split their donations among all potentially successful candidates to get concessions from all sides.[32]

[31] The interested reader can prove this by differentiating $U_j = U_j(A) + U_j(B)$ and $D_j = D_j(A) + D_j(B)$ with respect to D_j, expanding $\dfrac{dU_j}{dD_j}$ as a sum of partial differentials, and making the proper substitutions.

[32] Alexander Heard, *The Costs of Democracy* (Chapel Hill 1960), 58–67. From Heard's data this seems to be most likely among the largest donors. But Heard also notes this tendency among state employees in Indiana—individuals who might be assumed to have relatively accurate information regarding the rewards of donating to both sides as well as relatively high stakes in these rewards.

Implications for the "Downsian Voter"

This formulation of the ordinary member's response to political competition differs fundamentally from the model of rational voting developed by Anthony Downs in his book *An Economic Theory of Democracy*.[33] There he constructed a model of citizen behavior in an elaborately and rigorously defined democracy. In cases where no costs were associated with the act of voting, Downs argued that a citizen will vote if and only if he feels that *his* vote will increase his expected-utility stream. And when there are costs associated with voting, the differences the individual voter expects to make by casting his vote must be large enough to outweigh these costs.[34] Thus, if the citizen finds one party repugnant and the other ideal, and yet feels that the outcome of the election is a foregone conclusion, he is likely not to vote.

Downs's model is a special case of our formulation. He assumes that the only form of donation the citizen can give is his vote and that the translation of votes into probability of victory can be accomplished by a particularly simple transformation rule. We would argue that *any* donation made to a leader and/or an opponent would have to be based on a similar calculation. Furthermore, we would hypothesize that contributions may be motivated not only by the belief that they will change the probability of the outcome of the contest between the competitors. Contributions may also be exchanged for alterations in the contestants' programs. This may be true even if donations are only in the form of votes. Thus, when contributions are votes, they may be "given to a fiduciary" who can then deliver some or all of them

[33] Downs, *op.cit.*
[34] *Ibid.*, 271–273.

to the politician who is willing to give the group of individuals the programs they want. Such a notion would allow one to explain the rise of interest groups even under conditions of perfect information, a phenomenon which Downs ruled out as an impossibility.[35]

THE REACTION OF THE LEADER

Just as the ordinary member of the social structure must adjust his behavior following the emergence of opposition, so must the political leader. In general, of course, the behavior of the leader will be predicated on equation 3.3 as discussed above. He will consider the possibilities of continued occupancy of his role, going into opposition, and leaving the arena of competition altogether. And he will attempt to maximize the utility he can derive from these three possibilities over time.

Because he is a member of the social structure, the leader will receive any collective goods supplied by the opposition leader. As a result, he may actually donate to the opposition leader, pay him taxes, and even receive contracts from the opponent. All these considerations can be incorporated into the equation that defines the utility which the leader obtains from the occupancy of his role by the inclusion of the term $U_A(L'_B)$. With the introduction of this term, A's utility function for the occupancy of the leadership role becomes:

$$U_A(L_A) = U_A(X_A) + \sum_{j=1}^{n} D_j(A) + \sum_{j=1}^{n} T_j(A)|$$
$$- (1 - b_A)[C(O_A) + C(X_A)] + U_A(L'_B) \qquad (3.16)$$

[35] *Ibid.*, 90–91. The notion of a fiduciary is also developed in Curry and Wade, *op.cit.*, 41–44. Their formulation differs from ours, however, since it is based on situations involving only private-good exchanges.

This equation differs from the formulation presented in Chapter One only by the addition of the final term. The introduction of competition adds new dimensions to the calculations of the political leader, however, and produces a variety of implications for the tactics he is likely to employ.[36] Several examples may help clarify this point.

The introduction of competition will produce new factors affecting the donations the leader can obtain from the ordinary members of the social structure. He may self-consciously alter his programs, for example, as a device to increase the size of his donations. Such a move could have the effect of reducing the ability of a competitor to obtain donations by promising to supply new collective goods. Note that this tactic may not work at all in the absence of competition in cases where the leader is acquiring a major portion of his revenues from taxation.

In the absence of competition, the leader who relies heavily on taxation as a source of revenue is unlikely to obtain any significant amount of donations. But this conclusion does not hold in the presence of political competition. Even in cases where the ordinary members are heavily taxed, some members may find the program offered by the opposition leader unappealing and contribute voluntarily to the incumbent to help insure his continued occupancy of the leadership role. Thus, the existence of an opposition may generate potential sources of revenue for the leader which he could not otherwise tap.

At the same time, the leader can react to competition on a direct basis, rather than through added efforts to

[36] With respect to many of the points discussed in this section, there may be a mirror-image effect. That is, the opposition leader may often be able to employ similar tactics against the incumbent leader.

acquire donations. For example, the leader may find it profitable to manipulate the benefits and costs accruing to his opponent. He may be able to reduce the attractiveness of the position of the opposition leader by imposing high sanctions on individuals who attempt to go into opposition. Or the leader may attempt to buy off opponents by offering them attractive rewards for renouncing political competition and retiring into private life. Both the extent and nature of competition could be significantly altered through the use of devices of this sort.

Modes of Competition

A mode of competition has been defined as the combination of tactics employed by all of the competitors in a competitive situation. Any individual competitor's tactics can be described in terms of the pattern of his actions and the resources he employs for competitive purposes. Thus, the mutual acceptance of a decision rule, as we use that concept on pages 78 and 79, is a special aspect of the more general category of modes of competition which are agreed upon by the competitors and which specify the set of resources required for victory in the competition.

The mode of competition is of great importance in competitive situations because it governs the transformation of various types of resources into probability of victory for the competitors. Thus, the prevailing mode of competition will define which resources are relevant to the competition and determine the exchange rate between a bit of any given resource and a bit of probability of victory. The mode of competition will therefore define the "haves" and the "have nots" in political terms. It will determine to whose actions the competitors will pay attention and to whose demands the competitors are likely to be responsive. It will shape the range of actions open to all members of the social structure in the effort to improve their political positions.

Note, however, that the mode of competition need not be assumed to be fixed in any competitive situation. That is, any mode of competition is subject to manipulation on the part of the members of the social structure, at least in principle. Each individual member will therefore approach the problem of manipulation in terms of a cost-benefit analysis based on his own role premise. As a result, efforts to manipulate the existing mode of competition will occur whenever anyone calculates that the benefits of such actions outweigh the costs. In these terms, a stable or fixed mode of competition can best be conceptualized as the limiting case in which no member of the social structure finds the manipulation of the mode expedient. This concept of stability may be used to define a continuum, therefore, so that any given competitive situation may be characterized by a mode of competition that is more or less stable.

CHAPTER FOUR

Some Consequences
of Political Competition

THE EXTENSION OF THE model to cover situations involving political competition makes it possible to derive some propositions about a number of phenomena of interest to students of politics.

THE USE OF RESOURCES IN COMPETITIVE SITUATIONS

The introduction of competition immediately generates new considerations affecting decisions by the members of the social structure concerning the use of their resources.

The Uses and Values of Resources

In discussing voluntary contributions on the part of members of a social structure in previous chapters, we have assumed that each individual manipulates his fortunes by engaging in exchanges with leaders and aspiring leaders. This is possible because the leaders and aspiring leaders are willing to make concessions in order to receive donations from the members. Any competitor may have two reasons for valuing the donations of the members. First, he may find them valuable in their own right.

Second, he may be able to use these donations in efforts to change his probability of victory in the political competition. Both of these factors may enter into the motivation of any given competitor. If an individual possessed such extensive resources that the additional resources at the disposal of other members of the social structure were trivial by comparison, he would have little incentive to seek the leadership position. Similarly, it is difficult to conceive of a situation in which a competitor possesses so many private resources that the donation of resources by the noncompetitors could not significantly alter his probability of obtaining a leadership position. As a result, *one would expect all competitors to be interested in making exchanges for the voluntary contributions of the members.*

Given the interest of the competitors in the resources of the members, each individual member will be in a position to receive some benefit in return for any donations he might make. Each individual may donate in order to: (1) increase the probability that a preferred competitor will be victorious or will remain in opposition, (2) advantageously affect the program of the competitor to whom he donates, or (3) advantageously affect the program of the competitor to whom he does not donate.[1] If the donor is reasonably sure that the resources he is donating will be employed to increase his preferred competitor's probability of victory, he may make the donation with no strings attached. Under a wide variety of circumstances, however, individual members will attempt to obtain some concessions from the competitor in exchange for donations and will become involved in bargaining with the competitors.

To the extent that donations are valuable to the re-

---

[1] Equations 3.14 and 3.15 are applicable to this question.

cipient in themselves and are therefore solicited in exchange for promises of program changes, the analysis set forth in Chapter One is relevant. The exchange rate for donations designed to affect any competitor's probability of victory, on the other hand, will be a function of the tactics employed by all of the competitors (i.e. the mode of competition). This is so because the prevailing mode of competition will determine each competitor's demand function for specific types of resources, and these demand functions will help set the value of any potential donation. The ability of any individual to manipulate his fortunes, therefore, will be partially determined by the prevailing mode of competition. It follows that all members of the social structure will have incentives to establish that mode of competition which yields them the best returns on their potential donations.

Extremist Political Movements

Recall equations 3.13 and 3.15, which govern the size of the donations an individual member is willing to give to an opposition leader. Many of the terms in these equations are not subject to direct manipulation on the part of an opposition leader. In his efforts to maximize his profits, the opposition leader, B, will be able to manipulate his program, $U_j(L_B)$, and the extent to which he is willing to make program concessions in exchange for donations. The opposition leader, B, will also be able to manipulate his actions on behalf of donors in his capacity of opposition leader, $U_j(L'_B)$, and the extent to which he is willing to make program concessions to donors with respect to the role of opposition leader. Nevertheless, he has no direct control over the donors' estimations of his probabilities of becoming the leader and remaining the opponent, $P_j(L_B)$ and

$P_j(L'_B)$. And he cannot manipulate in any direct fashion the utility a_j expects to receive from A, $U_j(L'_A)$ and $U_j(L'_A)$, or A's responsiveness to a_j's contributions to B.

Under these conditions, any opposition leader will be able to acquire resources through donations only by: (1) being responsive to the interests of the donors both as the opposition leader and as a potential leader, (2) differentiating his projected leadership program from that of the incumbent leader, or (3) supplying valued services as the occupant of the role of opposition leader. If a given opposition leader has a very low probability of acquiring the leadership position, however, there are several predictions we can make about his behavior. The opponent, B, will receive donations from a_j so long as the expression governing the size of a_j's donations is greater than zero. In his attempt to keep this expression greater than zero and thereby insure himself a continued stream of donations, we would expect B to concentrate on the terms that he can control directly. He could either formulate his program in such a way that a_j finds it attractive in the first instance—i.e. establish a high $U_j(L_B)$—or be responsive to demands made upon him by a_j in return for contributions. But in the latter case, B is handicapped by a $P_j(L_B)$ term that is close to zero since B's responsiveness only enters into a_j's utility function when it is multiplied by $P_j(L_B)$.

In a situation of this kind, B is likely to orient the actions he takes in terms of the leadership role in such a way as to maximize the surplus he can obtain while remaining in opposition. He will not be overly concerned with the implications of implementing the policies he proposes, therefore, and he will use policy promises freely to maximize his surplus. Thus, he will differentiate his program sharply from that of the incumbent leader in the hope of gaining donations from individuals whose utility would be greatly increased by the alternative program. In terms of equation 3.15, he would attempt to manipulate $U_j(L_B)$ to make it as large as possible in comparison with $U_j(L_A)$ for some subset of the members of the social structure. After selecting his program, however, he can be expected to become much less responsive to programmatic demands placed on him by donors.[2]

B's efforts to differentiate his program significantly from that of the incumbent leader, however, will severely constrain his action. A competitor who does not rely on continuous exchanges of policy promises for additional donations must maintain a highly consistent set of promises which are very sharply differentiated from those of the incumbent leader. The logical outcome of this process is the orientation of B's program toward a highly homogeneous group of supporters who share a consistent set of demands which are very different from those made by other members of the social structure.

Aspiring leaders who have a low probability of victory in the competition for the leadership position are likely, on the other hand, to have a higher probability of remaining opposition leaders. Under the circumstances, an opposition leader with a low probability of acquiring the leadership position may concentrate on obtaining donations for actions taken in terms of the opponent's role instead of (or in addition to) activities aimed at the acquisition of the leadership position. Such an individual might find it advantageous to provide a variety of services in exchange for the contributions required

---

[2] This stems from the fact that, for any member, the expected value of any program break is the product of the value of the concession and the probability of victory (assumed to be near zero).

to make it profitable for him to continue to occupy the role of opposition leader.[3]

Politicization[4]

An individual member of a social structure may donate to a competitor to increase the probability that his preferred competitor will be victorious in the competition for the leadership position or to insure that the competitor does not lose the role of opposition leader. These are the only types of donations which competitors can receive with "no strings attached." Other donations will require concessions from the competitor. It follows, then, that competitors will seek to obtain as much of their revenue as possible from individuals who donate on this

---

[3] The conclusions set forth in this subsection can be derived more formally through the use of differential calculus. Because they are somewhat lengthy and because the algebraic manipulation is not central to our argument, we leave these derivations to the interested reader. Note, however, that equation 3.15 is already in the proper form for most of the analysis in this subsection. Beyond this, there is one additional assumption that is required to complete the derivations. We assume that someone always occupies the leadership role. That is, $P_j(L_A) + P_j(L_B) = 1$. This means that $\dfrac{\partial P_j(L_A)}{\partial D_j(B)} = -\dfrac{\partial P_j(L_B)}{\partial D_j(B)}$ and therefore $\dfrac{dU_j}{dD_j(B)}$ can be arranged to contain a term which includes the difference between the utility the member derives from the two contestants, $\dfrac{\partial P_j(L_B)}{\partial D_j(B)} [U_j(L_B) - U_j(L_A)]$. Thus, with regard to this term in the equation, the member's donations can be seen to be a function of the degree to which the opponent has differentiated his program from that of the leader.

[4] The analysis here, in contrast to most of the other arguments in this book, will be based on changes in information conditions. That is, the interactions between the leader and the individual member in situations in which information conditions are subject to manipulation will be considered.

basis. Any donor who realized his potential bargaining power, on the other hand, would prefer to make his donations contingent on the receipt of an additional reflection of his interests in the substantive program of the competitor. As a result, if information conditions are subject to manipulation, each competitor will try to control information concerning his willingness to make deals with prospective donors. The competitors will do this to avoid pressures to make concessions in exchange for donations they might have received in any case. But the competitors will probably find it difficult to control the relevant information completely. That is, once an individual discerns that he can affect his fortunes by making donations, he is likely to continue to develop his political awareness further (i.e. to become more politicized). There are two ways in which he may develop such an awareness.

First, the competitor who receives a donation may inadvertently help the donor to realize that a *quid pro quo* can be extracted for any future donations. This stems from the fact that a competitor who receives an unsolicited donation with no strings attached knows that the donor places a positive value on his program. As a result, the competitor has a strong incentive to attempt to induce the donor to increase his contributions. That is, the competitor is likely to solicit donations from the same individuals who have previously contributed to him. If the competitor does not offer any concessions in exchange for further donations, there are three possible types of information that he can give the donor to induce him to increase his donations. The supply of information will elicit more donations only if it induces the donor to: (1) increase his valuation of the recipient's program in terms of both the leader's role and the opposition leader's role, (2) decrease his valuation of the

106

program of the recipient's opponent, or (3) increase his estimation of the efficacy of his donations in securing victory for the recipient or in helping the recipient avoid exclusion from the political arena. Efforts along these lines to elicit additional donations will often be profitable. Under the circumstances, the competitor himself will frequently disseminate added information concerning the efficacy of the members' donations. Such information is most likely to be supplied to individuals who have already expressed their preferences through donations. But, in general, the dissemination of such information will lead the donor to an appreciation of the value the competitor places on his donation. The donor will thus be led to the realization that he can request something in exchange for solicited donations.

Second, an individual who at first gave donations with no strings attached may learn of his potential bargaining power through the very mechanics of the act of donating. The act of donating may, for example, put the individual in contact with other donors, some of whom have already been able to strike bargains with the recipients. The act of donating, therefore, increases the chances that any given individual will discern that he can bargain with the competitors to whom he donates. As a result, the donor who gives initially simply to increase the probability that his preferred competitor will be victorious may soon turn into a more sophisticated political contributor.[5]

A more extended analysis of the process of politicization would carry us too far afield from the purpose of

[5] It may be interesting to compare our approach to the phenomenon of politicization with the analysis of Gabriel Almond and Sidney Verba, *The Civic Culture* (Princeton 1963). Their analysis would suggest that a process similar to the one we have described occurs in countries lacking a strong tradition of political participation on the part of the membership.

this book. Several specific conclusions concerning pol-iticization, however, can now be drawn from the model developed in the preceding chapters. First, individuals are likely to become progressively more politicized. That is, each political act is likely to increase their awareness of their political potential. This process is likely to be irreversible. Thus, without the introduction of repressive devices, individuals are likely to experience long periods of ever-increasing incentives to remain politically active. Second, the manipulation of information by the com-petitors is likely to be a crucial factor in determining the degree of involvement of individual members in the competition for the leadership position.

Stable Decision Rules

The analysis of competition in situations involving a stable decision rule will be complicated by the peculiar form of the transformation function of the resources in terms of which victory is calculated. The resultant com-plications can be seen with particular clarity when the decision rule specifies a single numeraire.[6]

In the absence of a decision rule, the transformation function turning resources into probability of victory will be continuous. That is, each additional bit of resource a competitor receives will bring him an added bit of probability of victory. Given the presence of a stable decision rule, however, the analysis will not follow these lines. Then, a fixed amount of the numeraire, by defini-tion, guarantees victory. If a given competitor has less than a minimum winning coalition, therefore, additional bits of the numeraire are important to him only insofar as he has some possibility of attaining a minimum

[6] The basic conclusions of this and subsequent arguments would hold even if the decision rule specified a set of numeraire resources.

winning coalition. As a result, a competitor who controls little of the relevant resource may find a small increment of this resource of almost no utility. Similarly, a competitor who already controls a minimum winning coalition may find added bits of the numeraire of no utility. These results follow because the transformation function for the numeraire has a discontinuity at the point of a minimum winning coalition. Contributions of the numeraire cannot be analyzed, therefore, in terms of continuous marginal analysis. And to the extent that other resources are directly translatable into the numeraire, they are also subject to this analytic limitation. The presence of "slippage" in the transformation of other resources into the numeraire, on the other hand, would mitigate the effects of this limitation.

One of the most striking consequences produced by a discontinuity of this kind concerns the premium competitors will place on getting resources committed to them on a firm basis. Under most conditions, competitors prefer to be certain of the resources at their disposal.[7] A special premium is placed on this kind of certainty, however, in cases where a decision rule exists. A defection of support from a competitor operating in a situation in which there is no decision rule would produce only the loss of the added bit of probability of victory represented by the resources withdrawn. Given the presence of a decision rule, on the other hand, a defection of support from a competitor controlling a winning coalition may cost him the certainty of gaining the leadership position, rather than just a marginal bit of probability of victory. Under the circumstances, one would expect competitors operating under a decision rule to place a

[7] Thomas C. Schelling has suggested a number of nontrivial conditions under which this generalization will not hold in his highly imaginative book *The Strategy of Conflict* (Cambridge 1960).

very high premium on firm commitments on the part of their supporters. In the United States Senate, for example, a behavioral norm that has often been commented upon concerns the importance senators attach to honoring commitments with respect to votes on bills.[8]

The importance of firm commitments of support has far-reaching implications for both the competitor and his supporters. The fact that the competitor needs to acquire firm or reliable support will give individual contributors more bargaining power than they would otherwise have. Potential supporters may calculate correctly that they can obtain particularly large concessions from a competitor if they offer him their support in the final stages of the competition, when he controls almost enough resources to guarantee victory. When there is a stable decision rule, therefore, potential supporters have incentives to hold out their contributions until the critical final stages of the competition.[9] In addition, there will generally be extensive strategic interactions among potential supporters who are seeking to place themselves in this favorable position. To offset this development, the competitor will offer favorable deals to those who give him their firm support at an early stage or try to convince potential supporters that he will offer the same concessions in exchange for a given donation at all stages in the competition.

One consequence of this argument is that competitors will have incentives to manipulate information regarding

[8] An analysis of the Senate which deals with this phenomenon as well as a variety of other consequences of fixed decision rules can be found in Donald R. Matthews, *U.S. Senators and Their World* (New York 1960).

[9] A factor that may mitigate this effect is the danger that a potential donor will be left out of the winning coalition altogether if he waits too long to offer his support.

110

their strength at every stage in the search for resources. Thus, each competitor will attempt to convey the impression that the contribution of the next supporter is distinctly useful but not absolutely essential to ensure his victory. In addition, it follows from our argument that under most conditions competitors will seek to build coalitions larger than the minimum winning size so that defection on the part of the largest individual contributor would still leave the coalition equal to or greater than the size of a minimum winning coalition.[10] The padding of a coalition along these lines would allow the competitor a measure of invulnerability to blackmail threats from individuals who might demand added concessions in exchange for promises not to defect.[11]

This argument would explain some tendency on the part of competitors to seek coalitions that are larger than the minimum winning size. Another characteristic of competition for political leadership positions, however, leads us to expect an even stronger tendency in this direction. Many of the *quid pro quo* exchanges that will be obtained from any given aspirant by his supporters will relate to the supply of collective goods. And to the extent that bargains involve exchanges of collective goods coming from the competitor for private goods that come from the supporters, the competitor will have less incentive to minimize the size of his winning coalition. For insofar as collective goods are supplied by competitors in contests for political leadership positions, the re-

---

[10] In terms of this discussion, the exception would be a case in which the competitor had perfect information and the individual donors were able to make absolutely binding commitments.

[11] Such defection requires that there be some lag between the time resources are promised and the time they are delivered. But this is in fact the case in most empirical situations.

111

sultant situations are not zero-sum in character. What one supporter gains need not be a loss for another, and the pressure to minimize the number of individuals who will enjoy the fruits of victory is reduced. In addition, it follows from this argument that if a competitor promises to supply a certain collective good in exchange for donations from a given supporter, he will have every incentive to hide this fact from as many people as possible to obtain additional support by promising to supply the same collective good to other individuals. In analyzing the programs of political entrepreneurs, therefore, a careful distinction must be drawn between those policies that deal with the distribution of private goods (e.g. tax laws) and those that deal primarily with collective goods (e.g. constitutional questions).[12] Any analysis that fails to take this distinction into account will miss a number of the critical aspects of political competition.[13]

From the perspective of the individual supporter, there are several factors that help explain the dynamics of coalition formation and that bear on the final size of the winning coalition. An analysis of these factors yields an explanation of the phenomena of "peaking" and "bandwagon effects."

Consider first the phenomenon of "peaking." In a protracted competition for resources, potential donors are

[12] Although it can be argued that David Easton's well-known definition of politics in terms of the authoritative allocation of values for a society subsumes this distinction, neither Easton nor those who have adopted his definition have pursued the implications of this distinction. See David Easton, *The Political System* (New York 1953), esp. Chapter V.

[13] William Riker's *The Theory of Political Coalitions* (New Haven 1962) is a clear-cut example of the limitations arising from the failure to make the distinction between private and collective goods. Riker is prevented from drawing this distinction because he deals almost entirely with zero-sum conditions.

continually acquiring new information concerning the amount of resources that the competitors have at their disposal. Each competitor will attempt to create the impression that he is becoming progressively stronger and will soon attain the critical mass of resources necessary for victory. Under these conditions, individuals donating their resources are likely to feel that additional contributions on their part will be efficacious in increasing the probability that their preferred competitor will be victorious.

If individuals are making donations to increase the probability that their preferred aspirant will be victorious, there is a danger that the impression of momentum, which the competitor seeks to communicate, will get out of control with unwanted consequences for him. Thus, whenever the ordinary members acquire the impression that one competitor already controls sufficient resources to assure victory, they will be unwilling to make additional contributions to his cause, which they will view as costly and inefficacious. If such an impression of sure victory becomes widespread sometime before the decision rule is applied, the competitor in question may suffer a sharp decline in the flow of contributions to his cause. This decline may become so sharp that he will in fact be denied his anticipated victory. In such cases, the competitor can be said to have "peaked" too early. It follows that competitors will always seek to avoid giving contributors who make non-*quid-pro-quo* donations the impression of certain victory prior to the application of the decision rule.

When donations are based primarily on *quid-pro-quo* exchanges involving program concessions, the phenomenon of a "bandwagon effect" may occur. Any uncommitted contributor will maneuver in order to place himself in a position in which he can obtain the greatest

113

concessions from the competitor he ultimately backs. As mentioned previously, this is most likely to occur if the contributor pledges his support during the final stages of the competition. That is, despite all disclaimers on the part of the competitors, they are likely to make the greatest concessions for the support of those individuals who are in a position to offer their support at a crucial moment. As it becomes apparent that one of the competitors is approaching the point at which he will command a winning coalition, individuals interested in concessions from him in exchange for their contributions will rush to his support. They will be concerned lest he obtain the necessary resources to assure victory without their help and, hence, be unwilling to offer them concessions in return for their contributions. To the extent that such individuals are concerned with the potential rewards they can obtain from the victor, then, we would expect a stampede to support any competitor who is showing great strength. This would be so even if it appeared that he was already "over the top." Such actions will not necessarily be futile since competitors will usually seek to construct coalitions that are larger than the minimum winning size. All these factors will contribute to the generation of "bandwagon effects."

Under the circumstances, it might be asked what prevents the bandwagon effect from drawing the support of all members to the victorious competitor. There are two major constraining factors: the prospect of future political competitions, and the possibility of gaining concessions from the losing competitor in his capacity as the opposition leader.

Opposition and Exploitation

Even if an opposition is assured in a given social structure, the members will not necessarily benefit from the presence of opposition. Only if the opposition leader relies on voluntary contributions, in contrast to taxes, may members expect to benefit from the existence of continuous opposition. An opposition leader who does not need to take account of the preferences of the members in formulating his program will not necessarily safeguard the members from exploitation.[14] Members may in fact be subjected to exploitation by the opposition leader as well as the incumbent leader.

It may appear at first that the presence of a stable decision rule (which allows for continuous opposition because it specifies a numeraire resource that is different in kind from those resources required for the supply of collective goods) will tend to decrease the probability that the members will be exploited. But this will not necessarily be the case for any particular individual. Any decision rule not only defines the resources in terms of which victory in the competition for the leadership position will be calculated, it also helps to determine the value of other types of resource in exchanges between competitors and contributors. In so doing, however, the decision rule will determine which resources will not be demanded by the competitors. Thus, the decision rule will contribute to the definition of the political "haves" and "have nots" in a social structure. As a consequence,

---

[14] As has been pointed out, there are various sources of capital available to competitors. Not only can the competitors rely on taxes rather than donations, they may also employ their own private capital. Neither of these options will necessarily produce benefits for the members of a social structure with the introduction of competition. Similarly, it can be shown that opposition funded by sources outside the social structure does not guarantee the accrual of any benefits for the ordinary members from the introduction of political competition. A formal proof of this last point, however, would require a more complicated model.

it will help to determine those who will be forced to pay if the competitors rely on taxes for their revenue, as well as those who will be able to achieve their objectives readily through voluntary exchanges if the competitors rely on donations. Under these circumstances, the presence of a decision rule will not only make the exploitation of some individuals probable, it will also determine those individuals who will be most susceptible to exploitation. Thus, while a decision rule may increase the bargaining strength of some members in their interactions with the leader and the opposition leader, it will tend to decrease the bargaining strength of others.

This double-edged quality of a decision rule leads us to an examination of the consequences of decision rules based on universal and equal suffrage, which are common in democracies. Such rules have often been suggested as guarantees of political efficacy and, therefore, minimum exploitation of the members of the social structure. That is, each individual is assumed to be able to protect his own interests under such an arrangement by exchanging his vote for policy accountability on the part of the leader. But this conclusion appears to be highly unsatisfactory since the transformation function that translates the numeraire (i.e. votes) into probability of victory is discontinuous under such a decision rule. Given this discontinuity together with an even distribution of the numeraire, it is virtually certain that no single individual can be sure that a donation on his part will be needed by any particular competitor. As a result, the individual will usually be unable to get much in exchange for his vote since a single vote will only produce a small incremental increase in the probability of victory for any competitor. It follows that the competitors will generally focus on bargains for resources that can be translated into substantial blocs of the numeraire.

Several significant conclusions about democratic politics flow from this argument. First, there is great potential in democracies for the profitable establishment of organizations, composed of subgroups of the general membership, capable of withholding and delivering large blocs of the numeraire. Similarly, an ability to control other relevant resources in large quantities is sure to be potentially profitable in the resultant political competition.[15] Under these conditions, the individual who holds a single unit of the numeraire and is not a member of any political organization is likely to assess his situation correctly as one of alienated inefficacy. Second, insofar as it is easier to control large quantities of relevant resources other than the numeraire, a system in which political campaigns are financed through donations may insure the domination of a plutocracy and, therefore, the exploitation of those members who do not belong to this plutocracy.

SOME COMPARISONS BETWEEN ECONOMIC AND POLITICAL COMPETITION

We turn now to a comparison of competition among suppliers of private goods and competition among suppliers of collective goods. To this end we will focus on the cases of economic competition within a single market and direct opposition to an incumbent political leader.

Opposition and Profits

Efforts to nurture an appearance that competition exists may be profitable for both economic and political

[15] The analysis of a fiduciary constructed by R. Curry and L. Wade is interesting in this connection (*op.cit.*, esp. 41–44). Note, however, that their analysis applies only to exchanges based on private goods and to certain types of democracies.

117

entrepreneurs. That is, both types of entrepreneur will often find it valuable to establish a "false" or "dummy" competitor. Only a political entrepreneur, however, will ever find it profitable to encourage the emergence of a genuine opposition (i.e. one that might actually jeopardize his own continued occupancy of the leadership role). Why is this so?

The establishment of a "false" competition is a common phenomenon in private-good markets. Suppliers of private goods frequently attempt, through the manipulation of information and in other ways, to induce consumers to think that they are actually receiving a different product if they buy one brand rather than another, even though both are marketed by the same supplier. Such a strategy may, for example, ensure that there is no room for a genuine competitor to enter the market since there are already so many "different products" on the market. Similarly, a social leader may find the establishment of a "false" opposition useful in maximizing his profit from the leadership role. Thus, he may find that by setting up a "false" opposition he can collect additional donations indirectly from members who support that opposition. And, just as with economic entrepreneurs, such a strategy on the part of the leader may make it more difficult for a genuine competitor to establish himself.[16] In these ways, the situations faced by the political and economic entrepreneurs are analogous.

However, the political leader, unlike the economic entrepreneur, can increase the revenue he receives from *his own* supporters by setting up a "false" competitor. This is so because the existence of competition may constitute a threat to the individual member of the group since the member cannot exclude himself from the col-

[16] This is the basis for the well-known ploy of introducing a stalking-horse in political campaigns.

lective consequences of the competitor's program. This being the case, the profitability of this strategy need not be a function of the "falseness" of the opposition.

Thus, under some conditions, the emergence of a genuine opponent will enable the incumbent leader to collect increased donations to compensate for the concomitant decline in the probability of the leader remaining in office over time. Thus, encouraging the emergence of genuine opposition can be a viable strategy only for the supplier of collective goods but not for the supplier of private goods. In the case of private goods, the introduction of competition in a given market is not threatening for the individual consumer. The buyer can simply refrain from purchasing goods from the competitor if he so desires. Only in the case of collective goods can proposed changes in program be threatening to the individual member since each member of the social structure must receive any collective goods supplied whether he wishes to or not. And since he cannot avoid the consequences of competition for the supply of collective goods, the individual member will be motivated to donate to ensure the victory of his preferred competitor and minimize the chances of victory of others. Under the circumstances, an incumbent leader may gain additional donations from the introduction of opposition whenever the members of the social structure prefer his program to that of the competitor. If the individual member can exempt himself from the effects of the leader's program (a possibility not yet introduced in this model), the emergence of an opponent with a less desirable program may fail to call forth increased donations for the incumbent leader.

Empirically, however, we would expect leaders to attempt to increase their profit by encouraging the development of genuine opposition only in situations where they have no other viable strategies. This is so because such a strategy will generally be a risky business: the increased donations must be perceived to be sufficient to offset the decrease in the leader's probability of staying in office.

Dual Entrepreneurs

The chief executive of a large, modern corporation may appear at first glance to be an ideal example of an economic entrepreneur. In fact, economists have attempted to analyze the behavior of such individuals primarily in terms of the classical assumption of profit maximization for the firm. But they have generally found explanations along these lines seriously deficient in empirical terms. The reason for this deficiency may be the omission by these traditional economic analyses of an important aspect of the executive's behavior. It is true that the basic profitability of the executive's role derives from the sale of private goods by his firm. The policies that determine the profitability of the firm, however, are collective goods for the firm's stockholders. As the individual who sets these policies for the firm, therefore, the chief executive is a political entrepreneur as well as an economic entrepreneur.

Such an individual is likely to be faced with competition from two sources. Insofar as his firm is supplying private goods at a profit, he must expect the emergence of competing firms anxious to capture some of his firm's profit. Such competition would be of the traditional economic variety. Since the executive is deriving profit from his role as the supplier of collective goods to the stockholders of his own firm, however, there may well be incentives for an opposition to arise to compete for the stockholders' support. As a result, various individuals may attempt to displace him by soliciting support from some or all of the stockholders. This may well account for such well-known phenomena as proxy fights in large corporations.

In the case of public-stock corporations, a decision rule is generally established which specifies the resources necessary to acquire or retain the leadership position. A majority of the votes cast at a given stockholder's meeting, for example, is a common rule. This will eliminate the possibility of successful opposition in cases where the chief executive holds or controls a majority of the shares in the corporation. Where no one controls a majority of the votes, on the other hand, the existence of such a rule makes opposition based on donations (i.e. votes) possible.[17]

This distinction between corporate executives who control sufficient blocs of shares to ensure their own tenure and those who do not suggests a conclusion concerning the behavior of executives. One would expect chief executives who control their own tenure to conform more closely to the traditional economic model based on the assumption of profit maximization. On the other hand, executives who do not control their own tenure may be expected to exhibit behavior that conforms more closely to that of a political entrepreneur. This distinction is very suggestive concerning both the types of goods executives will supply and the dimensions of the groups to whom they will supply goods of any kind.

[17] See Chapter Three, pp. 59–60 on this point.

121

CHAPTER FIVE

Strategic Interaction

ALTHOUGH A NUMBER OF consequences have been deduced from the model set forth in this book, we have frequently had to conclude that a determinate solution for a particular problem would require an analysis of strategic interaction. Thus, decisions concerning donations for the provision of a collective good, modifications of programs in the face of opposition, competition or collusion with a leader who taxes, choices of competitive tactics, and the allocation of support among competitors for leadership positions are all subject to the impact of strategic interaction.

In this chapter, the occurrence of strategic interaction is shown to be a consequence of a specific set of assumptions. Accordingly, the indeterminacy associated with strategic interaction will be prominent in any model including such assumptions. It follows that a wide variety of models will be subject to the constraints introduced by the indeterminacies arising from strategic interaction.

THE BASES OF STRATEGIC INTERACTION

Define strategic behavior as the behavior of an individual member of a group involving a choice of action contingent upon that individual's estimate of the actions (or choices) of others in the group, where the actions of each of the relevant others are based upon a similar estimate of the behavior of group members other than himself. The set of such behavior on the part of two or more interacting individuals will be referred to as strategic interaction.[1]

This definition of strategic interaction subsumes as a special case situations in which only two individuals are involved. That is, whenever one individual's choice is contingent upon his estimate of the actions (or choices) of only one other individual, who likewise finds his choice contingent upon an estimate of the first individual's choice, a special and limited form of strategic interaction occurs. The only difference between the general case of strategic interaction and the special, two-actor case, however, is that in the latter each individual must estimate the behavior of a single specified individual while in the general case each individual must estimate (and ultimately aggregate) the behavior of a number of relevant others, all of whom find themselves in symmetrically interdependent positions with respect to their choices. It is possible that bargaining as a response to the occurrence of strategic interaction will be less extensive in situations involving large numbers of individuals than in those involving only a few due to problems of communication and identifying explicit opportunities for bargaining. But this in no way suggests that the phenomenon of strategic interaction itself will cease to occur in situations involving large numbers of participants.[2]

[1] It is apparent that the concept of individual choice is central to the meaning of strategic interaction. In this book, we assume that an individual makes a choice whenever he selects a particular alternative from any set of differentiated alternatives.

[2] The connection between strategic interaction and information conditions should be stated explicitly. Strategic interaction is incompatible with the presence of perfect information along all dimensions. If an individual possessed such information, he could predict the probable choices of relevant others with complete accuracy, just as if the choices of these others were no longer contingent upon his own choices.

123

Given this definition of strategic interaction, it is possible to prove the following theorem:

ANY MODEL USED TO EXPLAIN THE SUPPLY OF COSTLY COLLECTIVE GOODS CANNOT PROVIDE A DETERMINATE SOLUTION WITHOUT SOLVING SPECIFIC PROBLEMS OF STRATEGIC INTERACTION IF THE MODEL IS BASED ON ASSUMPTIONS THAT INCLUDE THE FOLLOWING:

1. Individuals exist,[3] and these individuals receive the collective good if it is supplied;
2. Each individual exhibits the following characteristics:

    a. he perceives and evaluates alternatives;

    b. he estimates the probable choices of others (given each of his own possible actions) whenever such choices by others would affect his evaluation of his own alternatives;

    c. he incorporates any probabilities estimated in accordance with assumption 2b into his evaluation of his own alternatives;

    d. his valuation of an additional unit of a collective good changes as a function of the amount of the good supplied;

    e. he chooses among his alternatives on the basis of his evaluation of the alternatives.

The proof of this theorem is relatively straightforward. Since the collective good is costly, its supply will require the utilization of costly resources. By assumptions 1 and

---

[3] For ease of exposition we have stated this theorem and the discussion that follows in terms of individuals as actors. But the results need not be restricted to individual actors. A model involving any behaving units that manifest the characteristics listed in the theorem will be subject to the limitations specified.

2a, the necessity of using costly resources means that each member of the group will be confronted with a set of alternatives differentiated in terms of the amount of resources he contributes. The individual member's evaluation of each of these alternatives will be determined by the amount of the collective good he might receive as a result of choosing that alternative relative to the cost to *him* of the alternative. The amount of the collective good he actually receives, however, will be determined by the aggregate of the contributions made by all the members of the group. This follows from the collective nature of the good in question. By assumption 2b, therefore, each individual estimates the probable contributions of others. And these estimates of the probable contributions of others, along with the marginal condition (assumption 2d), will determine the value each individual calculates he will receive in return for his own contribution under each of his specific alternatives (assumption 2c). Thus, each individual's evaluation of his alternatives is a function of his assessment of the probable behavior of a subgroup excluding himself but containing all the other members of the group, and the evaluations of alternatives made by each of the others are similarly contingent upon estimates of the probable behavior of subgroups containing the first individual. If the group contains only two members, the relevant subgroups will both be single-member subgroups. When the group contains more than two members, on the other hand, both the number and the size of the subgroups will increase proportionately. In both cases, however, all the members of the group will find themselves in interdependent situations with respect to the evaluation of their alternatives. By assumption 2e, the evaluation of alternatives must determine each individual's actual choice among his alternatives. Each individual's choice

125

is therefore contingent upon his assessment of the actions (or choices) of the others. Symmetrically, the choices of each of the others are contingent upon assessments of the probable behavior of a subgroup which includes the first individual, and the theorem is proved.

In the specific model set forth in this book, we have assumed the existence of individuals who receive the costly collective goods. We have assumed that these individuals experience decreasing marginal utility from additional amounts of these goods. And we have assumed that such individuals act rationally and evaluate their alternatives in expected-utility terms, on the basis of the probabilities they assign. It should be clear that these assumptions subsume the conditions necessary for the proof of the theorem. As a result, strategic interaction must be taken into account in analyses of the problems of supplying collective goods based on this model.

In the absence of a solution to the problem of strategic interaction, therefore, it is not possible to reach determinate solutions concerning the behavior of groups with respect to the supply of collective goods. This is not to say that the individual members of groups do not ultimately come to grips with the problem of strategic interaction in their own decision-making. In fact, they must do so in order to make any decisions concerning their contributions toward the supply of collective goods (including the decision not to contribute). Moreover, there are several conceivable ways of dealing with the problem of strategic interaction in analytic terms. Thus, the problem can be handled through the introduction of any of a number of types of assumption. For example, it is possible to assume that in group situations displaying specified characteristics individuals always estimate the probable behavior of others in a certain way. As discussed in Chapter One, this approach has been taken by a number of previous theorists who have drawn an analogy between the supply of collective goods in large groups and the operation of perfect-competition markets in classical economics.[4] Similarly, it is possible to assume that the estimates individuals make of the probable behavior of others follow some probabilistic law. That is, individuals may come to any of a number of conclusions about the probable contributions of the relevant others with specified probabilities. The fact is, however, that at the present time we are devoid of laws concerning the relevant human behavior with respect to the supply of costly collective goods. Rather than introducing a set of arbitrary assumptions, therefore, we have emphasized the indeterminacies that are a necessary consequence of the present state of our knowledge concerning the supply of collective goods.

It should also be clear at this point that the indeterminacy of the model set forth in this book is characteristic of the entire family of models dealing with the supply of collective goods which allow for strategic interaction: all those models that conform to the conditions stipulated in the theorem. But any model that attempts to explain the supply of collective goods on the basis of purposive behavior and that allows for any coordination whatsoever between individuals (whether tacit or explicit) must conform to the conditions stated in the theorem. That is, an examination of the assumptions required to prove the theorem shows that none of them can be relaxed without a fundamental change in the problem under analysis.

Assumption 1 is required if any problem is to be stated in terms of the concept of collective goods. There are only two ways in which this assumption could be relaxed.

[4] For the details see Chapter One, pp. 20–21.

Either the supply of a collective good can be seen solely as a function of the behavior of some individual who does not receive the good, or the recipients can be viewed collectively as a single organism whose behavior explains the supply of the good to its constituent units. In the first case, the supply of any collective good reduces to the supply of an externality of the behavior of the non-recipient unit. This changes the problem from the analysis of the supply of collective goods to an analysis of whatever it is in terms of which the collective good is an externality. In the second case, the problem is changed to the acquisition of a private good by a single organism, thereby avoiding (by assumption) the whole phenomenon of collective goods.

Assumptions 2a and 2e are required for any model in which the supply of collective goods is assumed to be the result of purposive behavior. If the supply of a good comes about through an inadvertent selection of unperceived alternatives, the supply of the good cannot be the result of purposive action. Any such notion would produce a radical change in the problem at hand. Similarly, if the choice among alternatives is not contingent upon the evaluation of the alternatives, the resultant behavior cannot be construed as purposive.

Assumption 2c is necessary if the individual is to differentiate between risky outcomes and certain ones.

Assumption 2d is required to rule out the logical possibility that one individual will continue to supply a collective good indefinitely regardless of the activities of others, known or unknown to him. This assumption does not actually restrict the scope of the theorem since it is hard to conceive of an individual who has constant marginal returns with regard to the consumption of any good. We include it, rather, for the sake of logical completeness.

Finally, consider the implications of relaxing assumption 2b. What will happen if individuals do *not* assign probabilities to the possible actions of others? In such cases, individuals cannot incorporate any consideration of the intentions of others into their choices among alternatives. As a result, they can act only on the basis of the capabilities of others. It follows that no action can take place on the basis of cooperation or coordination. Thus, all individuals would have to act solely on an atomistic basis. Consequently, none of the problems of coordinated action, which are potentially of great importance in the supply of collective goods, can be analyzed in terms of models that relax assumption 2b.

Economists have been able to analyze a wide range of phenomena associated with the supply of private goods using models that do not require an assumption like 2b. That is, they have employed models involving atomistic or independent decision-making on the part of individuals. They have been most successful in explaining phenomena associated with situations in which coordination of effort is impossible (e.g., perfectly competitive market situations). In situations in which any coordination of effort is important (e.g., oligopolistic interaction and problems pertaining to the supply of collective goods), on the other hand, their success has been markedly diminished.

In summary, then, the assumptions underlying the theorem can be represented as follows: Any model designed to explain the conditions under which individuals will supply themselves with costly collective goods through purposive behavior, which allows them to distinguish between risky outcomes and certain ones in evaluating alternatives and incorporates any notion of coordinated effort must take into account the phenomenon of strategic interaction.

A COROLLARY

At this point we can state a corollary to the theorem:

ANY MODEL THAT CONFORMS TO THE ABOVE CONDITIONS AND THAT IS USED TO EXPLAIN COMPETITION FOR THE OCCUPANCY OF A ROLE IN TERMS OF WHICH A COLLECTIVE GOOD IS SUPPLIED WILL PRODUCE, AT SOME POINT PROBLEMS OF STRATEGIC INTERACTION.

The proof of this corollary is straightforward. As argued in Chapter Three, the provision of opposition to a leader who is supplying a collective good is itself a collective good for the members of the group. Thus, it follows directly from the theorem that analyses of the provision of competition for the occupancy of the leadership position will lead to situations involving strategic interaction.[5]

TYPES OF STRATEGIC BEHAVIOR

Strategic behavior will occur in the entire class of models that exhibit the conditions stipulated in the theorem, and several conclusions about the types of strategic behavior that will occur in such models can be offered.

[5] It often happens that opposition to an incumbent leader is organized by a group of individuals. To the extent that a group is involved in such activities, they involve efforts to secure victory for the group for whom the victory itself is a collective good. With respect to group competitors such as political parties, therefore, any model that personifies the group (i.e., treats it as a perfectly coordinated monolith) assumes away the entire process which determines the behavior of the group. There are numerous examples of such analyses in the field of political science. Perhaps the most well-known, formal model based on such assumptions, however, is the model developed by Anthony Downs in his book, *An Economic Theory of Democracy*. Downs assumes that political parties act as though they were single individuals to maximize their probability of victory in elections.

First, strategic behavior in these models will in general be of the nonzero-sum variety. This follows directly from the concept of collective goods. Whenever collective goods are supplied, *all* members of the group will receive them. Under these conditions, situations in which the gains and losses of the participants sum to zero are not likely to occur. This does not mean that the mix of competition and cooperation in strategic interactions involving collective goods cannot vary considerably. But it does mean that there will virtually always be some element of cooperation in such situations.

Second, strategic interactions in the models defined by the theorem will generally involve more than two actors. In noncompetitive cases, the strategic interactions will involve the leader and the members of the group. This allows for two types of strategic interaction: (1) the leader may interact with the individual members, and (2) the individual members may interact among themselves. In competitive cases, on the other hand, strategic interactions will involve the leader, opposition leader, and members of the group. Here four types of strategic interaction are possible. In either case, the strategic interactions can of course be collapsed to two-person situations, but only through the inclusion of additional assumptions. Thus, in noncompetitive situations, the ordinary members of the group can be treated as a collective actor interacting with the leader. And in competitive situations, the members of the group can be viewed as constituting the environment in which a two-person interaction between the leader and the opposition leader takes place.[6] In both cases, however, the

[6] This assumes that there is only one opposition leader. In cases involving several opposition leaders, N-person interactions would occur, and the problems of coalition formation would become important.

131

two-person interaction will take place within the context of a larger N-person interaction.

Some of the simpler analyses of strategic interaction associated with zero-sum, two-person game theory, therefore, are not likely to be adequate in dealing with the types of strategic interaction discussed in this chapter. This by no means suggests that these problems cannot be analyzed successfully. It does indicate, however, a distinct need for more advanced forms of strategic analysis to handle the types of problems associated with the models defined by the theorem.[7]

[7] Oran Young is dealing with these problems in his current work.

CHAPTER SIX

Conclusion

IN THE PRECEDING CHAP-
ters, we have analyzed each of the issues raised in the
Introduction to this essay. As it stands, however, the
theory is restricted in several important respects. Even
though we have already been able to generalize the initial
model considerably, the limitations on the theory as
formulated in this book are still substantial. Nevertheless,
there is no need for the model to be confined to its
present form. In this final chapter, therefore, we wish
to identify clearly the principal limitations on our theory
in its present form and to comment on the prospects
for reducing or eliminating them in future work based
on the theory.

CURRENT LIMITATIONS AND DIRECTIONS
FOR THE FUTURE

First, the theory assumes that individual utility functions remain stable over a period of time. This is not
only a matter of preference orderings among known alternatives, it is also a question of the emergence of previously unknown options. As a result, the theory cannot
be employed to analyze the transformation of values or
utility functions, a process that is sometimes thought to
be a central feature of economic and political modernization. While it would be possible to modify the assumption of stable utility functions in certain ways, this

assumption cannot be relaxed entirely within the framework of the theory of politics presented in this essay.[1]

Second, though the theory demonstrates the importance of strategic interactions in a large class of situations, it does not arrive at determinate solutions for the strategic problems associated with the supply of collective goods. At best, it defines the variables in terms of which strategic interactions will occur and shows that the strategic interactions associated with the supply of collective goods will generally be of the nonzero-sum and N-person variety. But this allows us only to conclude that the simpler forms of strategic analysis associated with two-person, zero-sum game theory will be inadequate to deal with the strategic problems arising in our model. Under the circumstances, it seems clear that the analysis of more complex forms of strategic interaction represents one of the major challenges for the future in the study of politics.

Third, the present version of our theory is limited by the fact that it offers only a preliminary analysis of the intervening variable of modes of competition. Two areas in particular remain to be explored in this connection. In the first instance, it would be possible simply to assume different modes of competition and to examine the resultant differences in political competition. A brief start has been made in this direction in the discussion of decision rules and numeraire resources in Chapter Four. Beyond this, it would be interesting to consider the possibilities of analyzing the manipulation of modes of competition in more detail.

Fourth, a rather specific *information condition* has been used in developing the theory. It is clear that the

---

[1] Note that this limitation is common to all theories that are based on the assumption of rational choice.

availability of information is an important factor underlying a number of the conclusions we derive from our model. Accordingly, it would be useful to reconsider a number of the questions dealt with in this book on the basis of different available information. A wide range of interesting, though often complicated, questions would be generated by movement in the direction of less perfect information. The analysis of politicization in Chapter Four constitutes one example of the kinds of question that would emerge in this context.

Fifth, it was assumed at the outset that contributions for the supply of collective goods would come from those who received the goods. Thus, nonrecipients would not contribute to the supply of collective goods received by others. Although this may be a perfectly reasonable assumption in many situations, it actually defines a special case. In extreme situations, a collective good may be paid for entirely by a nonrecipient who does so as a side effect of his other behavior.

Sixth, our analysis of political competition is fully applicable only to situations involving collective goods that exhibit jointness of supply and that are not affected by crowding. We believe that such "pure" cases are of considerable interest, especially as a place to begin in the analysis of collective goods.[2] Nevertheless, it is clear that collective goods of this kind constitute a special case. We feel that efforts to extend the model through the relaxation of these conditions will offer a fruitful channel for future work. The problems raised by crowding effects

---

[2] On this issue we follow the position of Paul Samuelson rather than that of Julius Margolis. Compare the articles cited earlier in the *Review of Economics and Statistics* by Samuelson, "The Pure Theory of Public Expenditure," and "Diagrammatic Exposition of a Theory of Public Expenditure," and by Margolis, "A Comment on the Pure Theory of Public Expenditure."

appear to be less difficult in analytic terms, but also less fundamental, than the problems associated with jointness of supply.

Seventh, we have not dealt in any formal fashion with variations in the membership of social structures. That is, groups have been defined by the supply of some set of collective goods which are coextensive. No exclusion mechanisms, such as those on which private-good exchanges are based, are posited. Under these circumstances, there can be no ambiguity about membership since all those who receive the set of collective goods are automatically classified as members of the social structure, while nonrecipients are simply not members. But these assumptions define a special case. The situation becomes more complicated when there are several distinct collective goods and when the possibility of manipulable exclusion mechanisms is allowed. In the case of multiple collective goods, the groups formed by the recipients of the various goods may not be entirely overlapping or coextensive, with the result that it becomes difficult to determine membership in the social structure in any straightforward fashion. The problem of exclusion mechanisms, on the other hand, arises when an individual can be prevented from receiving a collective good that is being supplied and that he would in fact receive except for some manipulable barrier. Examples of such mechanisms would include dues for membership in a club, tolls for the use of a highway, a decoding device to receive the signals from a lighthouse, and fees to operate a pay phone. It is at this point that the problems of collective goods and private goods begin to merge. Finally, in the most general case, it would be possible to have situations involving noncoextensive groups and manipulable exclusion mechanisms at the same time.

These phenomena raise several problems that have

not been treated extensively in the present book. To begin with, there is the question of defining the membership and delineating the boundaries of social structures. This perspective also opens up the questions of entry and exit with respect to membership in social structures. In addition, the whole problem of subgroups comes into focus at this point. It is apparent that the phenomenon of subgroups, referred to from time to time in previous chapters, raises questions that will require extensions of our present theory to permit analysis of them. The limitations under discussion here, therefore, are relatively severe ones. Nevertheless, it is our feeling that these questions constitute a stimulating challenge for the future and that additional work in this area may prove especially rewarding in terms of theoretical payoffs.

Extensions along these lines would make it possible to employ the theory of the supply of collective goods to deal with a number of specific problems that have long been of interest to students of politics. An analysis of political leaders who make a profit by directing their activities toward some subgroup within a social structure, for example, could be carried out on a formal basis from this perspective. Similarly, the study of subgroups would make it possible to deal with hierarchical relationships among political leaders in a social structure. This would raise interesting questions about such topics as the interactions among national, state, and local leaders. Finally, the demarcation of distinct subgroups within an overarching social structure would allow for the analysis of interactions among groups on a horizontal or equal basis. This would generate a number of interesting questions about international relations as well as about intranational relations among leaders at the same level in the political hierarchy, such as mayors of cities or governors of states.

137

RECAPITULATION OF PROPOSITIONS

In the preceding section, we have argued that the theory set forth in this book casts up a wide range of questions that require further analysis. We wish to conclude, however, by reemphasizing the fact that we have already been able to derive a number of propositions from the model in its present form. For convenient reference, the most important of these propositions are listed here, along with references to the pages in the text where they are discussed.

1. Some individuals will occupy leadership roles even though they do not place a positive value on the collective goods in question. (8)

2. A political leader will change his position on specific substantive issues whenever he can increase his leader's surplus by doing so. (8)

3. The incentives for nonleaders to compete for a leadership role increase as the leader's surplus expands. (9)

4. Competition will be supplied only when some individual finds it profitable to do so. (9)

5. Institutions exist which supply collective goods to large groups entirely on the basis of donations. (21–22)

6. Some individuals who value a collective good more than the cost of providing it will not contribute toward its supply. (23)

7. The proportion of donations stemming from the members' desire for increased contracts will increase as a function of the degree of specialization of production in a society. (37–38)

8. Owners of specialized factors of production will compete for adoption of programs that utilize their factors by making donations to the leader whenever alterna-

tive collective goods being considered for inclusion in the leader's program require different factors of production. (38)

9. In the absence of competition, the amount of donations (other than those for contracts) a political leader receives will vary inversely with the amount of taxes collected. (50–54)

10. Whenever there is competition for a leadership role, the chances of an aspirant's being successful will increase as a function of the size of his valuation of the administrative aspects of his role. (46–47)

11. Whenever the overall economy grows faster than the public sector, leadership recruitment will shift toward the lower-income strata of the society. (48–49)

12. To the extent that economic development leads to an increase in the size of the public sector of the economy relative to the private sector, competition for political leadership roles will become more broadly based as a society undergoes the process of modernization. (48–49)

13. Political entrepreneurs will diversify with respect to both the supply of collective goods and their sources of revenue as a function of the presence of organizational complementarities in their operations. (54–55)

14. The more a political leader depends upon donations, the more wary he will be of collective goods that are durable or have high initial costs of supply. (55–56)

15. A political entrepreneur will diversify his activities more and more into the provision of private goods as the size of his overall operation increases (within a single social structure). (58)

16. Collective goods will never be optimally supplied. (59–62)

17. The supply of collective goods which exhibit no crowding effects will generate natural monopolies. (66–72)

18. Competition among suppliers of collective goods that exhibit jointness of supply and no crowding effects will not take the form of efforts to vie for shares of the market. (66–72)

19. In large groups, the greatest profit in the supply of any collective good will come from the first units of the good supplied. (69–72)

20. The larger the group, the less the overall quantity of the good supplied will change with any given fluctuations in the costs of supply. (69–72)

21. The maximum surplus a political leader can receive from supplying a collective good is a function of the number of people who consume the good. (69–72)

22. A politician will deliberately shorten his tenure in office whenever the immediate gains of doing so exceed the expected gains of remaining in office for a longer period. (82–83)

23. Opposition will never be optimally supplied. (84)

24. Some leaders will donate to an opposition leader, pay him taxes, and/or receive contracts from him. (96)

25. The introduction of opposition generates new sources of potential revenue for the incumbent leader. (97)

26. If his chances of victory are near zero, an opposition leader will differentiate his program sharply from that of the incumbent leader, and/or plan his actions to maximize the surplus he can obtain from remaining in opposition. (102–105)

27. Supplying information will elicit more donations only if it induces donors to: increase their valuation of the recipient's program; decrease their valuation of the program of the recipient's opponent; or increase their estimation of the efficacy of their donation in securing victory for the recipient or helping the recipient avoid exclusion from the political arena. (106–107)

28. The more an individual donates, the more likely he is to realize that he can bargain with the competitor(s) to whom he donates. (107)

29. Competitors operating under a decision rule will place a higher premium on firm commitments on the part of their supporters than those who do not. (109)

30. The introduction of a decision rule generates incentives for potential supporters to withhold their contributions until the critical final stages of the competition. (110)

31. To offset this development, competitors will offer favorable deals to those who give them their firm support at an early stage in the competition. (110)

32. A competitor will always attempt to convey the impression that the contribution of the next supporter is distinctly useful but not absolutely essential in insuring his victory. (111)

33. Unless they have perfect information and ironclad support, competitors will always seek to build coalitions larger than the minimum winning size. (111–112)

34. Whenever a competitor makes a definite promise to supply a collective good in exchange for contributions from a given supporter or group of supporters, he will try to hide this fact from as many people as possible. (112)

35. Competitors will always seek to avoid communicating an impression of certain victory to contributors who make non-*quid-pro-quo* donations prior to the application of the decision rule. (113)

36. As it becomes apparent that one of the competitors is approaching the point at which he will command a winning coalition, individuals interested in concessions from him in exchange for their contributions will rush to his support. (113–114)

37. The presence of a decision rule will not only make

the exploitation of some individuals probable, it will also determine those individuals most susceptible to exploitation. (115–116)

38. There is a great potential in democracies for the profitable establishment of organizations (composed of subgroups of the general membership) capable of withholding and delivering large blocs of the numeraire. (117)

39. The easier it is to control large quantities of relevant resources other than the numeraire, the more likely it is that a system in which political campaigns are financed through donations will lead to the domination of a plutocracy and, therefore, to the exploitation of those outside that plutocracy. (117)

40. Economic entrepreneurs who control their own tenure will conform more closely to the traditional economic model, based on the assumption of profit maximization, than those who do not. (121)

Appendices and Index

APPENDIX 1

The Size of Groups

THE QUESTION OF GROUP
size has arisen at several points in our discussion. It
seems desirable, therefore, to spell out in some detail
our reasons for deemphasizing the distinction between
small groups and large groups which Olson stresses so
heavily. In brief, Olson argues that both the likelihood
of approaching optimality in the level of supply of a
collective good and the probability of containing or limiting free-rider tendencies (in the absence of coercion or
positive, private-good incentives) decrease as the size
of a group increases. He cites three lines of argument
in support of this conclusion:

First, the larger the group, the smaller the fraction
of the total group benefit any person acting in the
group interest receives, and the less adequate the re-
ward for any group-oriented action, and the farther
the group falls short of getting an optimal supply of
the collective good, even if it should get some. Second,
since the larger the group, the smaller the share of
the total benefit going to any individual, or to any
(absolutely) small subset of members of the group,
the less the likelihood that any small subset of the
group, much less any single individual, will gain
enough from getting the collective good to bear the
burden of providing even a small amount of it; in
other words, the larger the group, the smaller the likelihood of oligopolistic interaction that might help ob-

tain the good. Third, the larger the number of members in the group, the greater the organization costs, and thus the higher the hurdle that must be jumped before any of the collective good at all can be obtained. For these reasons, the larger the group, the farther it will fall short of providing an optimal supply of a collective good, and very large groups normally will not, in the absence of coercion or separate, outside incentives, provide themselves with even minimal amounts of a collective good.[1]

The first argument cited by Olson does not yield the conclusion he draws without the introduction of a further assumption. Although it is true that the larger the group the smaller will be any individual's fraction of the total group benefit associated with any collective good, this does not suffice to demonstrate that the supply of such goods in large groups will be suboptimal or nonexistent. As we argued in Chapter One, the conclusion that suboptimality will increase with group size only holds when arrangements for marginal cost sharing by the recipients of the collective good are ruled out.[2] And more generally, whenever marginal-cost-sharing arrangements are possible, it is not the size of an individual's fraction of the group's benefit which will determine his action. Rather an individual will decide on the size of his contribution for the provision of a collective good on the basis of an expected-utility calculation of his benefits.

[1] Mancur Olson, Jr., *The Logic of Collective Action* (Cambridge 1965), 48.

[2] Although the idea of marginal-cost-sharing arrangements is not stressed in *The Logic of Collective Action* (see pp. 30–31), it is introduced as a device for overcoming suboptimality of supply in Mancur Olson, Jr. and Richard Zeckhauser, "An Economic Theory of Alliances," in Bruce M. Russett, ed., *Economic Theories of International Politics* (Chicago 1968), 28–33.

This calculation will be based not on his fraction of the group's benefits but on the actual value to him of the good (or some change in the quantity of the good supplied), the probability that it will be supplied, and the cost to *him* of providing it. He will of course consider the benefits he might obtain were others to provide the good at some level with little or no cost to him, and he may make efforts to bargain in the hope of persuading others to bear most of the cost of the good. In general, however, these factors will not vary directly with group size. A rational individual, therefore, will not necessarily be less likely to contribute toward the supply of a collective good as the size of his group increases. Consequently, one cannot conclude from Olson's first argument that collective goods are less likely to be supplied or less optimally supplied in large groups than in small groups.

The second line of argument is dependent upon the first for its validity. Thus, Olson argues that the larger the group, the smaller the fraction of the group's benefits any small subset is likely to receive, and the less likely they are to act independently of the other members of the group to supply the collective good. But as we have already argued, this line of reasoning does not hold without the introduction of an assumption to the effect that no marginal-cost-sharing arrangements are possible. A small subset of members, just as an individual, will take concerted action to supply the good only if they feel they can thereby maximize their expected utility from the good. They will base this calculation on their estimation of the impact of their donations on the supply of the good. And given the possibility of marginal-cost-sharing arrangements, their willingness to contribute on this basis will not, in general, decrease with increasing group size.

147

Olson's third argument is based on the premise that the costs of organizing a group will go up as the number of members increases. But this line of reasoning does not justify the conclusion he draws from it. In general, it does not automatically follow that the costs of the supply of a collective good will be a function of the number of recipients. Thus, given the proper co-ordination and collection mechanisms, it is conceivable that a large group will be highly efficient in this respect. Moreover, it is not the absolute cost of organization that is crucial in determining whether a group can supply itself with a collective good. Only when the cost of providing a collective good to an additional member of a group (including the cost of coordination and collection mechanisms) is greater than the marginal contribution the additional member might make for the provision of the good does a serious problem of organization arise. And there does not appear to be any a priori reason to assume that this condition will be especially common in large groups, except in cases where there are severe "crowding effects." Although there may sometimes be a certain "lumpiness" in organizing large groups, therefore, the argument based on organization costs does not justify the conclusion that large groups will show a tendency not to supply themselves with collective goods.

There are two other formulations of the distinction between small and large groups with respect to the supply of collective goods. First, the distinction might be based on the notion of interacting utilities. In short, it seems reasonable to assume that interactions among the utility functions of individuals will be more probable in small groups than in large groups. Thus, in a small group each individual's utility may be significantly boosted through vicarious enjoyment of his fellows' well-being or lowered as a consequence of his fellows' suffering.[3] Such interactions would increase the utility payoffs any individual would receive from contributing to the supply of a collective good. And the effect would be greater, the smaller the size of the group. Thus, the smaller the group, the higher the probability that it would succeed in supplying the collective good to itself.

Although such an assumption of interacting utilities preserves Olson's distinction between small and large groups, the theoretical costs of relying on it are high. The logic of collective action, as presented by Olson, is based on the notion of rational self-interest. And the idea of interacting utilities goes squarely against the notion of self-interest as employed by most writers (including Olson). Some means of reconciling the two assumptions, therefore, would be required to maintain the consistency of the analysis.

Second, the distinction between small and large groups might be based upon the acquisition of information when information is imperfect and costly to obtain. For example, if a collective good is to be provided by some collective mechanism within a group, the cost of obtaining information about cheaters (those who do not do their share, whatever it may be) will generally decrease as the size of the group decreases.[4] And the lower the information costs, the higher the probability that cheaters will be sanctioned successfully. Each individual member of the group will consequently have a lower incentive to cheat, and the probability that the collective good

---

[3] Olson seems to come close to this notion in his discussion of "social incentives" (*The Logic of Collective Action, op. cit.*, 60–65). But he fails to draw attention to the consequences of introducing the problem of interacting utilities.

[4] Olson himself appears to have somewhat similar factors in mind in his discussion of the costs of organization for a group (*ibid.*, 46–48).

149

will be successfully supplied will increase. Under certain conditions, therefore, it is possible to argue that small groups will enjoy a comparative advantage in providing collective goods. But it should be stressed that this in no way implies that the supply of collective goods will be impossible or even improbable in large groups.

Table of Symbols

The following standard mathematical symbols are used in the text:

$\sum_{j=1}^{n}$ The sum of all indexed variables immediately following. For example: $\sum_{j=1}^{n} D_j(A)$ is the sum of donations made by all members of the social structure to A: $D_1(A) + D_2(A) + \ldots + D_j(A) + \ldots D_n(A)$.

d The d represents an infinitesimal change in the variable immediately following. For example, $dD_j(X_i)$ represents an infinitesimal change in the member a_j's donations for the provision of the collective good X_i.

$\dfrac{\partial}{\partial}$ The rate of change of the variable in the numerator with regard to the variable in the denominator, with all other variables held constant. For example, $\dfrac{\partial U_j}{\partial D_j(A)}$ represents the rate of change of a_j's utility with regard to donations to A, $D_j(A)$—all other donations held constant.

The following notation is used throughout the text:

A The occupant of the leadership role.

a_j A member of the social structure.

b The proportionality constant representing the proportional utility derived from administration. For example $b_A[C(O_A) + C(X_A)]$

151

represents the utility A receives from administration of the collection organization he controls and the collective good he supplies and $b_B[C(O_B) + C(X_B)]$ represents B's utility from presiding over his collection organization and collective goods.

B The occupant of the opposition role.

$C(\ )$ The cost of supplying whatever is included in the parentheses. For example, $C(X_A)$ represents the cost of supplying the collective goods, X_A, supplied by A.

$D_j(\ )$ The donations made by the member a_j to the individual or for the collective good represented in the parentheses.

E Exclusion from political competition.

E_A The exclusion of A from political competition.

E_B The exclusion of B from political competition.

E_{A+B} The exclusion of A or B from political competition.

$f_j(\ )$ The fraction of the contracts let to a_j by the individual represented in the parentheses. For example, $f_j(A)$ is the fraction of the contracts let by A to a_j.

L The leadership role.

L_A The occupancy by A of the leadership role.

L_{A+B} The occupancy of the leadership role by A or B.

L_B The occupancy by B of the leadership role.

L' The opposition leadership role.

L'_A The occupancy by A of the opposition leadership role.

L'_{A+B} The occupancy of the opposition leadership role by A or B.

L'_B The occupancy by B of the opposition leadership role.

O_A A collection organization supplied by the leader A.

$P_A(\quad)$ The probability A assigns to the occurrence of the event represented in the bracket. For example, $P_A(L_A)$ represents the probability A assigns to his occupancy of the leadership role.

$P_B(\quad)$ The probability assigned by B to the occurrence of the event represented in the parentheses. For example, $P_B(L'_B)$ represents the probability that B assigns to his occupancy of the opposition leadership role.

$P_j(\quad)$ The probability the member a_j assigns to whatever event is enclosed in the parentheses. For example, $P_j(X_i)$ represents the probability with which a_j expects to receive the collective good X_i.

r The prevailing profit rate for contracts in a social structure.

$T_j(\quad)$ The taxes paid by the member a_j to the individual represented in the parentheses. For example, $T_j(A)$ represents the taxes a_j pays to the leader A.

$U_A(\quad)$ The utility A receives from whatever appears in the parentheses. For example, $U_A(X_A)$ represents the utility A receives from the collective goods, X_A, he supplies.

$U_B(\quad)$ The utility B receives from whatever appears in the parentheses. For example, $U_B(X_A)$ represents the utility B receives from the collective goods, X_A, that A supplies.

U_j The utility derived by a_j, the jth member of the social structure.

$U_j(\quad)$ The utility the member a_j receives from whatever is in the parentheses. For example, $U_j(X_i)$

153

represents the utility a_j receives from the collective good X_i.

X_A The collective goods supplied by the leader, A.

X_B The collective goods supplied by the opposition leader, B.

X_i A collective good.

Table of Equations

1.8 $U_j(L_A) = U_j(X_A)P_j(X_A)$
$+ f_j(A)\ r[C(O_A) + C(X_A)] - D_j(A) - T_j(A)$

1.9 $U_A(L_A) = U_A(X_A) + \displaystyle\sum_{j=1}^{n} D_j(A) + \sum_{j=1}^{n} T_j(A)$
$- [C(O_A) + C(X_A)]$

1.10 $U_A(L_A) = U_A(X_A) + \displaystyle\sum_{j=1}^{n} D_j(A) + \sum_{j=1}^{n} T_j(A)$
$- (1 - b_A)[C(O_A) + C(X_A)]$

1.11 $U_j(L_A) = U_j(X_A)P_j(X_A)$
$+ f_j(A)\ r[C(O_A) + C(X_A)] - D_j(A) - T_j(A)$
(restatement of 1.8)

2.1 $[C(O_A) + C(X_A)]$

2.2 $(1 - b_A)[C(O_A) + C(X_A)]$

3.1 $U_B = U_B(L'_B)P_B(L'_B) + U_B(L_B)P_B(L_B)$
$+ U_B(E_B)P_B(E_B)$

3.2 $U_B = \displaystyle\sum_{t=1}^{m} \Big(U_B(L'_B)P_B(L'_B)$
$+ U_B(L_B)P_B(L_B) + U_B(E_B)P_B(E_B) \Big)_t$

3.3 $U_A = \displaystyle\sum_{t=1}^{m} \Big(U_A(L_A)P_A(L_A)$
$+ U_A(L'_A)P_A(L'_A) + U_A(E_A)P_A(E_A) \Big)_t$

3.4 $U_B(L'_B) = U_B(X_B) + \displaystyle\sum_{j=1}^{n} D_j(B) + \sum_{j=1}^{n} T_j(B)$
$- (1 - b_B)[C(O_B) + C(X_B)]$

3.5 $\quad U_B(L'_B) = U_B(X_B) + \sum_{j=1}^{n} D_j(B) + \sum_{j=1}^{n} T_j(B)$
$$- (1 - b_B)[C(O_B) + C(X_B)] + U_B(L_A)$$

3.6 $\quad U_j(L) = U_j(L_{A+B}) = U_j(L_A)P_j(L_A)$
$$+ U_j(L_B)P_j(L_B)$$

3.7 $\quad U_j(L') = U_j(L'_{A+B}) = U_j(L'_A)P_j(L'_A)$
$$+ U_j(L'_B)P_j(L'_B)$$

3.8 $\quad U_j(E) = U_j(E_{A+B}) = U_j(E_A)P_j(E_A)$
$$+ U_j(E_B)P_j(E_B)$$

3.9 $\quad U_j = U_j(L) + U_j(L') + U_j(E)$

3.10 $\quad U_j = U_j(L) + U_j(L')$

3.11 $\quad U_j = U_j(L_A)P_j(L_A) + U_j(L_B)P_j(L_B)$
$$+ U_j(L'_A)P_j(L'_A) + U_j(L'_B)P_j(L'_B)$$

3.12 $\quad \dfrac{\partial U_j}{\partial D_j(A)} = 0$

3.13 $\quad \dfrac{\partial U_j}{\partial D_j(B)} = 0$

3.14 $\quad \dfrac{\partial U_j}{\partial D_j(A)} = \dfrac{\partial U_j(L_A)}{\partial D_j(A)} P_j(L_A) + \dfrac{\partial P_j(L_A)}{\partial D_j(A)} U_j(L_A)$
$$+ \dfrac{\partial U_j(L_B)}{\partial D_j(A)} P_j(L_B) + \dfrac{\partial P_j(L_B)}{\partial D_j(A)} U_j(L_B)$$
$$+ \dfrac{\partial U_j(L'_A)}{\partial D_j(A)} P_j(L'_A) + \dfrac{\partial P_j(L'_A)}{\partial D_j(A)} U_j(L'_A)$$
$$+ \dfrac{\partial U_j(L'_B)}{\partial D_j(A)} P_j(L'_B) + \dfrac{\partial P_j(L'_B)}{\partial D_j(A)} U_j(L'_B)$$

157

$$3.15 \quad \frac{\partial U_j}{\partial D_j(B)} = \frac{\partial U_j(L_A)}{\partial D_j(B)} P_j(L_A) + \frac{\partial P_j(L_A)}{\partial D_j(B)} U_j(L_A)$$

$$+ \frac{\partial U_j(L_B)}{\partial D_j(B)} P_j(L_B) + \frac{\partial P_j(L_B)}{\partial D_j(B)} U_j(L_B)$$

$$+ \frac{\partial U_j(L'_A)}{\partial D_j(B)} P_j(L'_A) + \frac{\partial P_j(L'_A)}{\partial D_j(B)} U_j(L'_A)$$

$$+ \frac{\partial U_j(L'_B)}{\partial D_j(B)} P_j(L'_B) + \frac{\partial P_j(L'_B)}{\partial D_j(B)} U_j(L'_B)$$

$$3.16 \quad U_A(L_A) = U_A(X_A) + \sum_{j=1}^{n} D_j(A) + \sum_{j=1}^{n} T_j(A)$$

$$- (1 - b_A)[C(O_A) + C(X_A)] + U_A(L'_B)$$

Index